The Taijiquan & Qi Gong Dictionary

D1563854

Angelika Fritz

The Taijiquan & Qi Gong Dictionary

Copyright (c) Angelika Fritz 2017

All rights reserved.

No part of this book may be reproduced or transmitted in any form or by any means without written permission from the author.

ISBN-13: 978-1546324102   ISBN-10: 1546324100

Disclaimer
This book is for reference and informational purposes only and is in no way intended as medical counseling or medical advice. The information contained herein should not be used to treat, diagnose or prevent any disease or medical condition without the advice of a competent medical professional. The activities, physical or otherwise, described in this material may be too strenuous or dangerous for some people and the reader should consult a physician before engaging in them. The reader is fully responsible for his or her own health and welfare. The author and publisher of this material does not accept responsibility for any injury, loss or damage which may occur through reading or following the instructions in this book.

Knowledge is a treasure,
but practice is the key to it.

Laozi

Introduction

Ever since I started learning Taijiquan and Qi Gong more than 10 years ago, I have been fascinated by all the different concepts, theories and ideas that I have discovered. However, I have also been very overwhelmed by all the strange Chinese words, movement names, Traditional Chinese Medicine details etc.

Even though one can search and find almost anything online nowadays, I still like to have a real book in my hands. Something I can look into whenever I have a question to get an immediate response; without having to look at a screen. Or a book to browse through and discover new words and concepts that I haven't heard of before.

Thus I had the idea to write a dictionary for Taijiquan and Qi Gong beginners and enthusiasts. As you can imagine the project got bigger and bigger. It also became more complex than I thought because there are words with different romanizations (like Tao and Dao). There are even words that look the same but might have a different Chinese pronunciation and mean something completely different (e.g. Zhong can mean "middle" or "heavy" or "loyalty", depending on the Chinese character).

I actually consider this dictionary a work in progress. Even though I have managed to cover many different entries I am sure there are many more that I could have added. And obviously one could write whole books about each entry. To list just a couple of words to explain "Qi" or "Yi" won't be satisfactory for advanced practitioners.

Therefore I strongly encourage you to work with this book. Write all your complementary thoughts into it. Add the words that are missing. Go into more detail for those things that are important to you. Share your insights with your fellow practitioners.

For example, you'll find many acupuncture points in the dictionary. If you want to get deeper into meridians (channels, vessels etc., I won't distinguish between them) then get a book and add the exact location of the acupuncture points. Or maybe you want to broaden the section about numbers at the end of the book. Or add the movements of your preferred Taijiquan form in Chinese.

Actually, as I wrote the dictionary, more and more questions arose for me. Taijiquan and Qi Gong give me an opportunity to learn for the rest of my life and I am looking forward to the journey of answering those questions.

So remember: talk to your teachers, your fellow students or even ask me to learn more. I surely do not grasp every detail fully and even after all the years with Taijiquan and Qi Gong, I still consider myself a beginner. But if you have any questions, ideas or additions, feel free to contact me via my blog about Taijiquan and Qi Gong: **Qialance.com**!

Angelika Fritz

A

Abdominal Breathing see: Fan Tong Hu Xi or Fu Shi Hu Xi.

Active Qi Gong see: Dong Gong.

Active Tuck in the Robes see: Huo Bu Lan Zha Yi.

Acupressure see: Dian Xue massage.

Acupuncture a key part of traditional Chinese medicine. It includes inserting fine needles into specific (acupuncture) points on the body, most of them lying on meridians. It is used for prevention and treatment of disease.

Acupuncture Point see: Xue.

Acquired Essence see: Postnatal Essence.

Adverse Climates see: Six Excesses.

Alchemy see: Lian Dan.

An (downward) push. A technique for pushing/striking the opponent. An is one of the postures of the Grasp Sparrow's Tail sequence and is one of the eight basic methods of Taijiquan (Ba Men).

Ancient Tree entwines its Roots see: Gu Shu Pan Gen.

Animal Head Pose see: Shou Tou Shi.

An Mo literally "Press Rub". Meaning ordinary massage (compared to Tui Na).

Ao Bu Twisted Step. A Taijiquan move. See also: Lou Xi Ao Bu.

Apparent Close-up or Appears Closed see: Rufeng Shibi.

Application see: Yong Fa.

Arahat see: Luohan.

Arc the Hands see: Gong Shou.

Aromatic Qi Gong see: Xiang Gong.

Arrange Legs to Split see: Bai Jiao Die Cha.

Art of War an ancient Chinese military treatise from the 5th century BC. Attributed to Sun Tzu.

Attack Ears with Both Fists see: Shuang Feng Guan Er.

Attack the Tiger see: Pi Shen Hu Fu.

Azure Dragon emerges from Water see: Qing Long Chu Shui.

B

Ba eight (8).

Ba Chu Eight Touches, also called Chu Gan (Touch Feel) or Dong Chu (Moving Touch). The phenomena and feelings one can experience during Qi Gong practice. The exact names of the sensations vary, some examples are Dong (moving), Yang (itching), Liang (cool), Leng (cold), Nuan (warm), Re (hot), Qing (light), Zhong (heavy), Se (harsh), Hua (slippery), Diao (shaking), Yi (rippling), Fu (floating), Chen (sinking), and Ruan (soft).

Backward Strike or Backward Thrust to Intimidate see: Ci Hui Yi Jun Chen Chi Ren Hun.

Backward Trick see: Hou Zhao.

Ba Duan Jin Qi Gong Eight Pieces of Brocade Qi Gong. One of the most common forms of Qi Gong, consisting of eight exercises. These lead to a silken/brocade-like quality of the body and its energy. Its creation is usually attributed to Yue Fei (1103-1142). Originally called Shi Er Duan Jin (Twelve Pieces of Brocade), it was later shortened to eight movements.

Bagua (also Pa Kua) Eight Trigrams, literally "Eight Divinations". In the book Yi Jing, eight basic principles are derived from Yin and Yang. These eight principles are each represented by three broken and/or straight lines known as (eight) trigrams. Their names are Qian, Dui, Li, Zhen, Xun, Kan, Gen, and Kun. In Taijiquan the trigrams correspond to the eight basic techniques: Peng, Lu, Ji, An, Cai, Lie, Zhou, and Kao (see also: Ba Men).

Baguazhang Eight Trigrams Palm. One of the internal Chinese martial arts, based on the Bagua theory. It emphasizes the application of palm techniques and circular movements. Its creation is attributed to Dong Hai-Chuan in the 19th century.

Bai hundred (100).

Bai Bu (also Pai Bu) Swing Step or Toe-out-step.

Bai E Liang Chi see: Bai He Liang Chi.

Bai He White Crane. A Shaolin Gongfu style which imitates the fighting techniques of the crane.

Bai He Liang Chi White Crane Spreads Its Wings. Also called White Goose Spreads Its Wings (Bai E Liang Chi). A Taijiquan move.

Bai Hui acupuncture point 20 on the Governing Channel (Du Mai 20), translated as Hundred Convergences. Also called Ni Wan Gong. It is located at the crown of the head, in line with the apex of the ears. It is an important point for good posture as it is the point where one should feel like one is suspended from heaven with a string.

Bai Jiao Die Cha Arrange Legs to Split or Swing the Foot and Drop Down. A Taijiquan move.

Bai Lian Sweep the Lotus or Swing over Lotus. A Taijiquan move.

Bai She Tu Xin White snake spits out tongue. A Taijiquan move.

Bai Shi (also known as Kowtow) the formal initiation ceremony conducted by a master in which one or more students "Enter the Door" and become disciples. See also: Ru Men.

Bai Yuan Bao Dao Wang Shang Kan White ape drags glaive and cuts upward. A Taijiquan move.

Bai Yuan Xian Guo (also: Yuan Hou Tan Guo) White ape presents fruit. A Taijiquan move.

Bai Yun Gai Ding White clouds cover the head. A Taijiquan move.

Balance Stance see: Du Li Bu.

Ba Mai see: Qi Jing Ba Mai.

Ba Men literally "eight doors". The eight basic moving patterns/techniques of Taijiquan: Peng, Lu, Ji, An, Cai, Lie, Zhou, and Kao. They are part of the thirteen powers of Taijiquan (Shi San Shi).

Ban (also Pan) to deflect.

Ban Lan Chui (also Pan Lan Chui) Deflect, Parry, Punch. A Taijiquan move.

Bao Hu Gui Shan Embrace the Tiger and Return to Mountain or Carry Tiger Back to Mountain. A Taijiquan move.

Bao Pu Zi literally "Book of the Master who embraces Simplicity". A Chinese book about Qi Gong, medicine and other topics, written by Ge Hong (283-343).

Bao Shen Mi Yao "The Secret Important Document of Body Protection". A Chinese medical book describing moving and standing Qi Gong practices, written by Cao Yuan Bai during the Qing dynasty (1644-1912).

Bao Tou Tui Shan Cover/Grasp/Embrace Head and Push Mountain. A Taijiquan move.

Ba Shi see: Ji Ben Ba Shi.

Basic Methods of Taijiquan see: Ba Men.

Beak Hand see: Gou Shou.

Beast Head Pose see: Shou Tou Shi.

Beating the heavenly drum see: Ming Tian Gu.

Beautiful Lady's Hand see: Fair Lady's Hand.

Beginning see: Qi Shi.

Beijing form see: 24 form.

Bei Zhe Kao Fold and Lean with Back. A Taijiquan move.

Belt Vessel see: Dai Mai.

Bend Bow Shoot Tiger see: Wan Gong She Hu.

Ben Lo see: Lo, Benjamin.

Bian Que (died 310 BC) according to legend the earliest known Chinese doctor. The book Nan Jing (Classic on Disorders) is attributed to him.

Bian Shi bian stones. The stones used to press acupuncture points before metal needles were available.

Big cloud hands and small cloud hands see: Da Gong Quan Xiao Gong Quan.

Bi Men Shi close the doors. A Taijiquan move.

Bing Bu Merging Step, means feet together.

Bi Qi Seal the Breath. A category in Qin Na techniques. These specialized techniques attack the breathing passages of the body.

Bi Shen Chui see: Pie Shen Chui.

Bi Xi Nose Breathing.

Black Bear rolls over its back see: Hei Xiong Fan Shen.

Black Bear turns backward see: Hei Xiong Fan Shen.

Black Dragon sways its tail see: Wu Long Bai Wei.

Black Tiger searches in the mountains see: Hei Hu Sou Shan.

Bladder Yang organ associated with the element Water. Short form Bl for Bladder meridian.

Blade falls into chest as you embrace the moon see: Lou Zai Huai Zhong You Bao Yue.

Blood see: Xue.

Blue Dragon sways its tail see: Qing Long Bai Wei.

Blue dragon turns over see: Qing Long Zhuan Shen.

Blue Dragon wags its tail see: Qing Long Bai Wei.

Blue-green (azure) dragon comes out of the waters see: Qing Long Chu Shui.

Bo Cao Xun She ploughing the grass and searching for a snake or parting the Grass looking for snakes. A Taijiquan move.

Bodhidharma see: Da Mo.

Body Unit see: Cun.

Bone Marrow Cleansing see: Xi Sui Jing.

Book of Changes see: Yi Jing.

Bow Stance see: Gong Bu.

Bo Cao Xun She Separate the Weed on the side to search for the Snake. A Taijiquan move.

Bo Yun Wang Ri Scatter the Clouds and See the Sun. A Taijiquan move.

Broadsword see: Dao.

Brocade Qi Gong see: Ba Duan Jin Qi Gong.

Brushing Foot see: Ca Jiao.

Brush Knee see: Chu Shou or Lou Xi.

Brush Knee and Step Forward see: Lou Xi Ao Bu.

Bu step, stance, footwork. Some of the most known stances are Ma Bu and Gong Bu.

Bubbling Well see: Yong Quan.

Buckle Step see: Kou Bu.

Buddha Hand see: Fo Shou.

Buddha's Warrior Attendant Pounds Mortar see: Jin Gang Dao Dui.

Buddhism a religion that encompasses a variety of traditions, beliefs and spiritual practices largely based on teachings attributed to the "Enlightened One", the Buddha. The Chan sect of Buddhism (pronounced Zen in Japanese) was established by the Indian monk Bodhidharma (Da Mo) in 520 AD in China.

Buddhist Breathing see: Fo Jia Hu Xi.

Bu Diu Bu Ding Don't lose contact and don't resist. A term in combat Taijiquan.

Bu Fa stepping exercises.

C

Ca Bu forward step, in which the heel skids forward.

Cai to pluck or to grab. A technique with pull down energy to unbalance the opponent. One of the eight basic methods of Taijiquan (Ba Men).

Cai Longyun (1929-2015) one of the creators of the Taijiquan 24 form.

Cai Xiao Yao literally "to pluck the little herb". A term used in Taoist Qi Gong practice.

Ca Jiao (also Tsa Jiao) Sweeping Kick or Brushing Foot or Rub with Foot. A Taijiquan move.

Calligraphy a visual art related to writing. Chinese calligraphy is widely practiced in China. It is one of the Five Excellences.

Cannon Bashing see: Er Lu.

Cannon Fist see: Er Lu.

Cantong Qi see: Zhou Yi Can Tong Qi.

Cao Cao (155-220) a Chinese historical figure portrayed in the Three Kingdoms novel.

Cao Yuan Bai a Chinese doctor and Qi Gong master. Author of the book Bao Shen Mi Yao (The Secret Important Document of Body Protection), written during the Qing dynasty (1644-1911 AD).

Carrying a Thousand Pounds see: Tuo Qian Jin.

Carry Tiger back to Mountain see: Bao Hu Gui Shan.

Cat Stance see: Mao Bu.

Ce Gong Bu side bow stance.

Central Guoshu Institute see: Zhong Yang Guo Shu Guan.

Cha Bu cross-step behind. See also: Gai Bu.

Chan a school of Buddhism combined with Taoism. Better known by its Japanese name Zen. It asserts that enlightenment can be attained through meditation, self-contemplation and intuition.

Chang long.

Chang Chuan see: Chang Quan.

Change Palms Three Times see: San Huan Zhang.

Chang Qiang acupuncture point 1 on the Governing vessel (Gv-1), translated as Long Strong. See also: Weigu.

Chang Quan Long Fist. A family of external martial art styles from Northern China.

Chang San Feng see: Zhang San Feng.

Chan Kam Lee (died in 1953) a Taoist teacher and Lee style Taijiquan master. His main disciple was Chee Soo.

Chan Lien Tieh Sui Pu Tiu Pu Ting a term referring to the sticking aspect or adherence in Taijiquan.

Chan Mi Gong a Qi Gong form created by Liu Han Wen in the early 1980s. It focuses on soft movements of the spine.

Channel see: Meridian.

Chan Si Gong Silk Reeling. Qi Gong exercises practiced often in Chen style Taijiquan.

Chan Si Jin Silk Reeling Skill.

Chan Zong Liu Zu "Six Ancestors of Chan". One of them is Bodhidharma (Da Mo).

Chao Tian Deng Raise a Lamp toward Heaven. A Taijiquan move.

Chao Yang Tian Homage to the Sun. A Taijiquan move.

Chao Yuan Fang (550-630) a Chinese doctor and Qi Gong master. He compiled the Zhu Bing Yuan Hou Lun (Thesis of the Origins and Symptoms of Various Diseases).

Che Bu step backward with the front foot.

Chee Soo (1919-1994) a British Lee style Taijiquan and Qi Gong master, disciple of Chan Kam Lee.

Chen sinking. See also: Ba Chu.

Cheng Bao tree hugging stance. A variation of Zhan Zhuang.

Chen Bin (born 1979) a Chen style Taijiquan master, son of Chen Zhenglei.

Chen Changxing (1771-1853) a Chen style Taijiquan master who taught the art to Yang Luchan.

Chen Fake (1887-1957) a Chen style Taijiquan master. Father of Chen Zhaoxu and grandfather of Chen Xiaowang and Chen Xiaoxing.

Cheng Manching (1902-1975) a Yang style Taijiquan master, who taught in the United States since the 1960s. He developed a shortened version of the long Yang form called 37 form. His top students, called "the Big Six", were Tam Gibbs, Lou Kleinsmith, Ed Young, Mort Raphael, Maggie Newman, and Stanley Israel. Cheng Manching was called "Professor" by his students and "Master of Five Excellences" due to his skills in Chinese medicine, Taijiquan, calligraphy, painting, and poetry.

Cheng Tinghua (1848-1900, also known as Cheng Yingfang) a Baguazhang master.

Cheng Ying Hao Pose like a Hero. A Taijiquan move.

Chenjiagou name of the village of the Chen family, where Chen style Taijiquan originated. It is located in the Chinese province Henan.

Chen Ji Ru a Chinese doctor who wrote the book Yang Sheng Fu Yu (Brief Introduction to Nourishing the Body) during the Qing dynasty (1644-1911 AD).

Chen Po (also Chen Tuan, died 989) legendary creator of Liu He Ba Fa Quan during the Song dynasty (960-1279).

Chen Qingping (1795-1868) a Chen style and Zhaobao style Taijiquan master.

Chen style Taijiquan the oldest of the Taijiquan family styles, developed by Chen Wangting. Current head of the family is Chen Xiaowang.

Chen Tuan see: Chen Bo.

Chen Village see: Chenjiagou.

Chen Wangting (1580-1660, also called Chen Zouting). A Ming dynasty general who founded Chen style Taijiquan in his home village Chenjiagou (Henan province).

Chen Xiaowang (born 1945) a Chen style Taijiquan master, grandson of Chen Fake and brother of Chen Xiaoxing. Currently head of the Chen family.

Chen Xiaoxing (born 1952) a Chen style Taijiquan master, grandson of Chen Fake and brother of Chen Xiaowang. Currently head instructor at Chenjiagou.

Chen Yanlin (1906-1980) a Yang style Taijiquan master. His books are well known, e.g. "Taiji compiled: The Boxing, Saber, Sword, Pole, and Sparring" (published 1943).

Chen Youben (ca. 19th century) a Chen style Taijiquan master. He is credited with the creation of the Xin Jia (New Frame), which is also known as Xiao Jia (Small Frame).

Chen Yu (born 1962) a Chen style Taijiquan master, son of

Zhaokui.

Chen Yu Xia (1924-1986) a female Chen style Taijiquan master. The only daughter of Chen Fake.

Chen Zhaokui (1928-1981) a Chen style Taijiquan master. Son of Chen Fake and father of Chen Yu.

Chen Zhaopi (1893-1972, also Ji Fu) a Chen style Taijiquan master, a close relative and student of Chen Fake.

Chen Zhaoxu (1912-1959) a Chen style Taijiquan master. Son of Chen Fake and father of Chen Xiaowang and Chen Xiaoxing.

Chen Zhenglei (born 1949) a Chen style Taijiquan master. Father of Chen Bin.

Chen Zouting see: Chen Wangting.

Chi see: Qi.

Chi Kung see: Qi Gong.

Chin advance. See also: Qianjing.

Chinese Medicine see: Traditional Chinese Medicine.

Ching see: Jing. Can also mean Classic or Book.

Ching Shen see: Jing Shen.

Chin Na see: Qin Na.

Chong Thrust Kick. A Taijiquan move.

Chong Mai Thrusting Vessel or Penetrating Vessel. It is one of the Eight Extraordinary Channels.

Chopping Hand see: Zhan Shou.

Chou see: Zhou.

Chronoacupuncture see: Zi Wu Liu Zhu.

Chuan see: Quan

Chu Gan literally "touch feel". See also: Ba Chu.

Chu Gin Soon a Yang style Taijiquan master, disciple of Yang Shou-Chung.

Chu Guiting (1892-1977) one of the creators of the 24 form.

Chui (to) punch.

Chu King Hung (born 1945) a Yang style Taijiquan master, disciple of Yang Shou-Chung.

Chung Mai see: Zhong Mai.

Chu Shou (also Lou Xi) Brush Knee. A Taijiquan move.

Ci Hui Yi Jun Chen Chi Ren Hun Backward strike or Backward thrust to intimidate. A Taijiquan move.

Circle Walking the main training method of Baguazhang.

Circling the Hip like a Millstone see: Mo Yao Dao Hui Tou Pan Gen.

Close/Closing Hands see: He Shou.

Close the doors see: Bi Men Shi.

Closing see: Shoushi.

Cloud Hands see: Yun Shou or Da Gong Quan Xiao Gong Quan.

Coccyx see: Weigu.

Conception Channel see: Ren Mai.

Conclude Taiji see: He Tai Ji.

Confucianism Chinese philosophy of humanism which concentrates on the world of the living rather than the spiritual needs or the next world. It advocates personal and governmental morality, justice, sincerity, moderation, and adherence to traditional values. See: Confucius.

Confucius (551-479 BC) a Chinese scholar, whose philosophy has significantly influenced Chinese culture. See: Confucianism.

Cong Nei Zhu Ji to build the foundation of health and longevity internally. See also: Cong Wai Jian Gong.

Cong Wai Jian Gong to build the physical strength externally. See also: Cong Nei Zhu Ji.

Cotton Boxing see: Mian Quan.

Cover and Block see: Gai Lan Shi.

Cover Head and Push Mountain see: Bao Tou Tui Shan.

Cover Stance see: Gai Bu.

Cover Step see: Gai Bu.

Cover the Back see: Hou Zhao.

Cover the Front see: Qian Zhao.

Creation Cycle a term within the Five Elements (Wu Xing) concept. Meaning that wood creates fire; fire creates earth/ashes; earth yields metal; metal becomes molten thus creates water; and water creates wood.

Crossed Glaive cuts Chest see: Shi Zi Dao Pi Kan Xiong Huai.

Crossed feet see: Shi Zi Jiao.

Crossed hands see Shi Zi Shou.

Cross kick see: Shi Zi Tui.

Cross-step behind see: Cha Bu.

Cross-step in front see: Gai Bu.

Crouch Step Astride the Tiger see: Xia Bu Kua Hu.

Crouch Step like a Snake creeping out from a house see: Yi Tang She.

Cultivation refinement of the character and spiritual development.

Cun Body Unit. An anatomical measure used to locate acupuncture points. One Cun is equal to the width of the second joint of the thumb. Three Cun are equal to the breadth of the second, third, fourth, and fifth fingers when held together.

Cuo Cu misplace the bones. A category in Qin Na techniques.

Cut the White Snake at the Waist see: Yao Zhan Bai She.

Cutting through the White Snake's Hip see: Yao Zhan Bai She.

D

Da strike, hit.

Dabao acupuncture point 21 on the Spleen meridian (Sp-21), translated as Great Embracement.

Da Cheng Quan see: Yiquan.

Da Gong Quan Xiao Gong Quan Strike with Full Arm, also called Waving Hands or Big Cloud Hands and Small Cloud Hands. A Taijiquan move.

Da Hu Shi Strike Tiger. A Taijiquan move.

Dai Mai Girdle/Belt Vessel. It circles the body starting back at the level of the third lumbar vertebrae, while at the front of the body it passes midway between the pubic bone and the navel. One of the Eight Extraordinary Channels (Qi Jing Ba Mai).

Da Jia Large Frame. A style of Chen style Taijiquan. There are two types of Da Jia: Lao Xia (old frame) and Xin Jia (new frame).

Da Lu Large Rollback. See also: Lu. Da Lu also refers to a two-person push hands exercise.

Da Mo (483-540) the Indian Buddhist monk credited for creating the Yi Jin Jing and Xi Sui Jing while at the Shaolin monastery. He is also known as Bodhidharma.

Dan Bian Single Whip. A Taijiquan move.

Dance of the Blossom see: Quan Wu Hua.

Dan Ding Dao Gong "Dao Training in the Elixir Crucible". A Taoist Qi Gong training method.

Dang Tou Pao Head strike Cannon Fists or Straight Punch on the Head. A Taijiquan move.

Dantian "Elixir Field", "Cinnabar Field". An energy center in the body which is important within TCM, Qi Gong, and internal martial arts, because it is able to store and generate Qi. There are three Dantians: Shang Dantian (upper Dantian, between the eyebrows), Zhong Dantian (middle Dantian, the solar plexus area), and Xia Dantian (lower Dantian, lower abdomen).

Dantian breathing see: Dantian Hu Xi.

Dantian Hu Xi Dantian breathing, meaning deep breathing.

Dantian Qi Qi that is stored in the Lower Dantian. Also called Xian Tian Qi (Pre-Heaven Qi).

Dan Zhong see: Tan Zhong.

Dao see: Tao.

Dao broadsword or sabre. A single-edged Chinese sword.

Dao Cha Dao Cha Double Forearm Punches or Spread Arms Twice and Strike. A Taijiquan move.

Dao Cha Bu Sneak Step.

Dao De Jing see: Tao Te Ching.

Dao Er Gong Double Forearm Punches. A Taijiquan move.

Dao Hong-Jing (456-536, also Tao Hung Ching) author of the book "Yang Shen Yan Ming Lu".

Daoism see: Taoism.

Daoist Breathing see: Ni Hu Xi.

Daoist Canon see: Daozang.

Daoist Sage see: Xian.

Dao Jia literally "Dao Family", meaning the religious forms of Taoism.

Dao Juan Gong Step Back and Repulse Monkey, also Stepping Backwards with Turning Arms. A Taijiquan move. See also: Dao Nian Hou.

Dao Juan Hong Step Back and Whirl Arms like a Coiling Thread. A Taijiquan move.

Daolu see: Taolu.

Dao Nian Hou (or Dao Nian Hong) Step Back and Ward Off Monkey. A Taijiquan move. See also: Da Juan Gong.

Dao Qi Long Riding Dragon Backwards. A Taijiquan move.

Dao Training in the Elixir Crucible see: Dan Ding Dao Gong.

Dao Wai Cai Yao "Herbs picking outside the Dao". A term in Taoist Qi Gong training.

Dao Yin (also Tao Yin) an ancient term for Qi Gong.

Daoyin Yang Sheng Gong Shi Er Fa 12 routines from Daoyin tradition. A Qi Gong form.

Daozang (also Taoist Canon) a collection of approx. 1,400 Taoist texts including commentaries, history, poetry, rituals, meditations, philosophy, and Qi Gong exercises.

Da Shou Yin Large Hand Stamp. A Tibetan meditation technique.

Da Wu literally "great dance". A Qi Gong form.

Dayan Qi Gong Wild Goose Qi Gong. A Qi Gong form.

Da Zhou Tian literally "Grand Cycle Heaven", also translated as Grand Circulation. In this Qi Gong training method Qi is circulated through the whole body.

Deflect see: Pan.

Deng Jiao Heel Kick.

Deng Yi Gen Heel Kick.

De Qi "to obtain Qi". The sensation of electrical tingling, numbness, soreness etc. at the meridian where an acupuncture needle is inserted.

Destruction Cycle a term within the Five Elements (Wu Xing) concept. Meaning that wood destroys earth; earth absorbs water; water destroys fire; fire destroys metal; and metal chops wood.

Detoction within Traditional Chinese Medicine, this is the process by which herbs are boiled and the remaining medicinal tea is used for health purposes.

Di Earth. Earth (Di), Heaven (Tian) and Man (Ren) are the "Three (Natural) Powers" (San Cai). See also: Tu.

Diagnosis there are four examination methods in Traditional Chinese Medicine: questioning, inspection, listening/smelling, and palpation. Special emphasis is laid on the inspection of the tongue, the palpation of the pulse at each wrist and the acupuncture points, the observation of the complexion and facial features.

Diagonal see: Xie.

Diagonal Bow Stance see: Xie Gong Bu.

Diagonal Flying see: Xie Fei Shi.

Diagonal Posture see: Xie Xing.

Diagonal Subdue Tiger see: Pi Shen Fu Hu.

Diamond Qi Gong see: Jin Gang Gong.

Dian Mai see: Dim Mak.

Dian Mo see: Dim Mak.

Dian Tou Nod the Head. A Taijiquan move.

Dian Xue see: Dim Mak.

Dian Xue Massage acupressure. A Chinese massage technique in which the acupuncture points are stimulated through pressing. It is the root of Japanese Shiatsu.

Diao shaking. See also: Ba Chu.

Die Cha Shake Foot and Stretch Down. A Taijiquan move.

Die Da bone-setting. The TCM practice for dealing with trauma and injuries such as bone fractures, sprains, and bruises.

Di Jiu Tiao Pao Meng Hui Tou Offer Wine – Pick up Cloak – Suddenly Turning Back. A Taijiquan move.

Di Li Shi Di Li = "geomancy", Shi = "teacher". A Feng Shui teacher or master.

Dim Mak literally "press artery" (Cantonese), also called Dian Xue, Dian Mai or Dian Mo. The art of attacking/ striking/grasping acupuncture points to immobilize, injure or kill the opponent.

Ding to stabilize or to fix.

Ding Bu Fixed Step or T-Step. Also used for on site-/fixed-step practice in Tui Shou.

Ding Dian literally "fixed point". Can be used to describe the "ending posture" or the static posture that ends a martial art technique or a Qi Gong movement.

Ding Shen Stabilize the Spirit.

Ding Shi posture holding or performing a form with holding postures.

Di Qi Earth Qi.

Disciple see Di Zi.

Di Zi (lineage) disciple. A student chosen to learn and to pass on the knowledge of a specific martial arts family or lineage.

Dojo Japanese term for a martial arts training hall. See also: Kwoon.

Dong moving. See also: Ba Chu.

Dong Chu literally "Moving Touch". See: Ba Chu.

Dong Gong Active/Dynamic/Moving Qi Gong. Qi Gong techniques that include movement. Opposite is Jing Gong.

Dong Hai-Chuan (1797-1882) a Chinese internal martial artist, credited as the creator of Baguazhang.

Dong Mian Fa Hibernation technique. A Qi Gong technique.

Double Forearm Punches see: Dao Er Gong or Dao Cha Dao Cha.

Double Jump Kick see: Ti Er Qi.

Double Pound Mortar see: Shuang Jin Jiao.

Double Raise Kick see: Er Qi.

Double Weighting see: Shuang Zhong

Double White Lotus see: Shuang Bai Lian.

Douglas, Bill (born 1957) founder of World Tai Chi Qi Gong Day.

Dou Jin shaking/trembling power or vibration technique. The internal martial art technique of shaking the body suddenly with great force.

Down xia.

Downward Single Whip see: She Shen Xia Shi.

Dragging the Waist and Hitting with the Elbow see: Yao Lan Zhou.

Dragon and Tiger Qi Gong a Qi Gong set.

Dragon hacks the ground see: Que Di Long.

Drill zuan.

Drop Stance see: Pu Bu.

Double Raise Kick see: Er Qi.

Duan short.

Duan Jin short power.

Dui one of the Eight Trigrams. See: Bagua.

Du Li Bu Single-Leg Stance or Balance Stance.

Du Mai Governing Channel. The main Yang meridian of Qi because it governs all of the Yang meridians in the body. Starting at the tip of the coccyx (tailbone) it travels up the mid line of the back, over the head, and descends from the crown down the front of the face, ending at the upper lip. It is one of the Eight Extraordinary Channels (Qi Jing Ba Mai).

Duqi navel.

Dynamic Qi Gong see: Dong Gong.

E

Eagle and bear fight see: Ying Xiong Dou Zhi.

Eagle and Bear Vie with their Wits see: Ying Xiong Dou Zhi.

Earth see: Tu or Di.

Earthworm burrowing under the mud see: Que Di Long.

E Hu Pu Shi Hungry Tiger attacks for Food or Hungry Tiger Pouncing on its Prey. A Taijiquan move.

Eight ba (8).

Eight Basic Methods of Taijiquan see: Ba Men.

Eighteen Movements see: Shibashi Qi Gong.

Eight Energetic Bodies the Taoist concept that a human being has eight vibratory frequencies of energy: physical body, Qi body, emotional body, mental body, psychic energy body, causal body, body of individuality and body of the Tao.

Eight Extraordinary Meridians see: Qi Jing Ba Mai.

Eight Guiding Principles the four diagnostic sets in TCM that define patterns of distress within the organism: cold-hot, deficient-excess, internal-external, Yin-Yang.

Eight Pieces of Brocade see: Ba Duan Jin Qi Gong.

Eight Stances see: Ji Ben Ba Shi.

Eight Touches see: Ba Chu.

Eight Vessels see Qi Jing Ba Mai.

Elbow Meets Fist see: Zhou Di Kan Quan.

Elbow (Stroke) see: Zhou.

Embrace Head and Push Mountain see: Bao Tou Tui Shan.

Embrace Tiger and Return to Mountain see: Bao Hu Gui Shan.

Embracing the Moon see: Huai Zhong Bao Yue.

Embryonic Breathing/Respiration see: Tai Xi.

Emei name of a mountain in Szechuan Province, China. It is one of the four sacred Buddhist mountains of China.

Emei Da Peng Gong a Qi Gong form from the Emei mountain in China.

Emotional Mind see: Xin.

Empty Stance see: Xu Bu.

Energetic Bodies see: Eight Energetic Bodies.

Entering Tranquility see: Ru Jing.

Extraordinary Meridians see: Qi Jing Ba Mai.

Er two (2).

Er Gong Forearm Punch. A Taijiquan move.

Er Lu second form. A Chen style Taijiquan form within the old frame (Lao Jia). Also known as Pao Chui or Cannon Fist.

Er Qi Double Raise Kick. A Taijiquan move.

Essence see: Jing.

Essence Doors see: Jingmen.

Exploring Wisdom Qi Gong see: Hui Gong.

External Kidneys see: Wai Shen.

External Martial Arts see: Wai Jia.

External Qi Healing see: Wai Qi Zhi Liao.

Extraordinary Vessels see: Qi Jing Ba Mai.

F

Fa method, way.

Fair Lady's Hand also Beautiful Lady's Hand or Fair Maiden's Hand. A typical hand position especially in the Cheng Manching 37 postures form.

Fair Lady works with Shuttles see: Yu Nü Chuan Suo.

Fajin (also Fa Chin) a technique in Taijiquan to issue energy/power explosively.

Falling Flowers see: Luo Hua Shi.

Falun Gong a Chinese spiritual practice that combines meditation and Qi Gong exercises with a moral philosophy.

Fan literally "return". See: Fan Xi.

Fan (weapon) see: Shanzi.

Fan Fu Hu Xi Reverse abdominal breathing. See also: Ni Hu Xi.

Fan Hu Xi see: Fan Fu Hu Xi.

Fan Hua Wu Xiou Overturning Flowers and Waving Sleeves. A Taijiquan move.

Fan Jing Bu Nao literally "to return the Jing to repair the brain".

Fan Shen Kan turning the body and performing a strike. A Taijiquan move.

Fang Song to loosen the body. Relaxation without softness.

Fang Song Gong Relaxation Qi Gong.

Fan Penetrates Back see: Shan Tong Bei.

Fan Shen Xia Pi Jian Turn around and Chop downward. A Taijiquan move.

Fan Shen Zai Ju Long Tan Shui Turn and Raise Glaive to Test the Water. A Taijiquan move.

Fan Through Back see: Shan Tong Bei.

Fan Tong Hu Xi Back to childhood breathing. See also Fu Ji Hu Xi.

Fan Xi Return Breathing, meaning to return to natural breathing.

Fa Qi to discharge/emit/issue Qi.

Feng Chi acupuncture point 20 on the Gallbladder meridian (Gb-20), translated as "wind pool". Do not mix up with Feng Shi!

Feng Fu acupuncture point 16 on the Governing channel (Gv-16), translated as Wind Mansion.

Feng Huang Dian Tou Phoenix Nods its Head. A Taijiquan move.

Feng Juan Can Hua Whirlwind Withers the Flowers. A Taijiquan move.

Feng Lu Wind Path. A meditation method.

Feng Shi acupuncture point 31 on the Gallbladder meridian (Gb-31), translated as "wind market" (do not mix up with Feng Chi!). In Wuji position (preparing or closing the form), the tip of the middle finger may touch this point.

Feng Shui literally "Wind-Water". The ancient art of geomancy (Di Li) and a Chinese philosophical system of harmonizing everyone with the surrounding environment (involving design and placement of buildings etc. according to the movements of Qi in the environment).

Feng Shui Shi literally "Wind Water teacher". see: Di Li Shi.

Fen Jiao Separate Foot or Separation Kick or Kick foot. A Taijiquan move.

Fen Jin Separate the Muscles. A category in Qin Na techniques.

Fen Sui Xu Kong Crush the Emptiness. A term in Taoist Qi Gong.

Fire see: Huo.

Fire Dragon Gong see: Huo Long Gong.

First Form see: Yi Lu.

Fishing the Moon Out from the Bottom of the Sea see: Hai Di Lao Yue.

Fist showing under the elbow see: Zhou Di Kan Quan.

Fist under Elbow see: Zhou Di Chui.

Five wu (5).

Five Animal Qi Gong see: Wu Qin Xi.

Five Elements see: Wu Xing.

Five Excellences Name for five Chinese arts: Chinese medicine, Taijiquan, Calligraphy, Painting, and Poetry. Cheng Manching was called "Master of Five Excellences".

Five Steps see: Wu Bu.

Fixed Step see: Ding Bu.

Flash the Back see: Shan Tong Bei.

Flat Stance see: Pu Bu.

Flesh-eating Demon explores the Sea see: Ye Cha Tan Hai.

Flinging Body Punch see: Pie Shen Chui.

Flower Step see: Hu Jiao Bu.

Fo Jia literally "Buddhist family", meaning Buddhist religion.

Fo Jia Hu Xi Buddhist Breathing, also called Zheng Fu Hu Xi.

Fold and Lean with Back see: Bei Zhe Kao.

Forearm Punch see: Er Gong.

Form see: Taolu.

Forming a Cross with the Halberd then Raise see: Shi Zi Yi Dao Wang Ju Qi.

Forming a Cross with the Halberd and Splitting the Heart see: Shi Zi Dao Pi Kan Xiong Huai.

Forward Step see: Ca Bu.

Forward Trick see: Qian Zhao.

Food Qi see: Shi Qi.

Fo Shou Buddha Hand. A Qi Gong hand form.

Four si (4).

Fragrance Qi Gong see: Xiang Gong.

Frame see: Jia.

Fu Yang Organs, also known as the "hollow" organs". Their task is to transform matter, liberate its essence, transport substance, and discharge waste. The Yang organs are the Bladder, Gallbladder, Small Intestine, Stomach, and Large Intestine. Though not an organ, the Triple Burner is also considered to be a Fu.

Fu floating. See also: Ba Chu.

Fu Hu Subduing the Tiger. A Taijiquan move.

Fu Ji Hu Xi literally "abdominal muscles breathing". A Qi Gong breathing technique, also called "Back to childhood breathing" (Fan Tong Hu Xi).

Full Martial Flower see: Quan Wu Hua.

Full Turn see: Quan Wu Hua.

Fu Qi Fa Yield Qi methods.

Fu Xi Skin Breathing. See also: Ti Xi.

Fu Zheng literally "to help/support what is correct". A term in Traditional Chinese Medicine to protect the immune system.

Fu Zhongwen (1903-1994) one of the creators of the Taijiquan 24 form.

G

Gai Bu Cross-step in front, also called Cover Stance or Cover Step.

Gai Lan Shi Cover and Block. A Taijiquan move.

Gallbladder Yang organ associated with the element Wood. Short form Gb for Gallbladder meridian.

Gang Bao Mian Hua Steel Wrapped in Cotton. Taijiquan is also referred to as Cotton Boxing (Mian Quan).

Gang Rou Xiang Ji "harmonious balance of toughness and tenderness", meaning when a martial arts practitioner uses hard and soft power together.

Gan Jue literally "feel conscious", meaning to feel, to become aware of, feeling and sense. It means to be able to feel what is going on inside your body. See also: Yi Shi.

Gao Tan Ma High Pat on Horse or Pat Horse on High Back. A Taijiquan move.

Gathering at the Knees see: Lou Xi.

Ge Hong (283-343) a doctor and Qi Gong master who wrote the book Bao Pu Zi.

Gen one of the Eight Trigrams. See: Bagua.

General Guan Carries Broadsword see: Guan Sheng Ti Dao Shang Ba Qiao.

General Guan carries his glaive to Ba Bridge see: Guan Sheng Ti Dao Shang Ba Qiao.

Ge Zhi Yu Lun "A Further Thesis of Complete Study" is a medical and Qi Gong thesis written by Zhu Dan-Xi (1281-1358).

Girdle Vessel see: Dai Mai.

Golden Bell Cover see: Jin Zhong Zhao.

Golden Cock/Rooster stands on one Leg see: Jin Ji Du Li.

Golden Elixir see: Jin Dan.

Gong an achievement or skill from effort, practice, hard work, and discipline.

Gong Bu Bow Stance. See also: Xie Gong Bu, Zheng Gong Bu, Yu Gong Bu.

Gongfu (Kung Fu) literally "energy-time", meaning supreme skill from hard work. Any study, art or practice that needs continuous time, labor, patience, and energy to complete and master. As Chinese martial arts require a lot of time and energy to master, they are often called Gongfu. However Gongfu is applicable to any mastery, e.g. music or calligraphy.

Gong Shou literally "to cup one's hands in obeisance or greeting". As a standing Qi Gong meditation form also called Arc Hands or Universal Post.

Gou Shou Beak Hand or Hook Hand.

Governing Channel see: Du Mai.

Grab see: Cai.

Grain Qi see: Shi Qi.

Grand Circulation see: Da Zhou Tian.

Grand Ultimate Boxing a name sometimes used for Taijiquan.

Grasping and Hitting see: Xiao Qin Da.

Grasp Head and Push Mountain see: Bao Tou Tui Shan.

Grasp Sparrow's Tail see: Lan Que Wei.

Great Dance of Qi Gong see: Da Wu.

Green/Blue Dragon Emerges from Water see: Qing Long Chu Shui.

Grinding Disk Sword see: Mo Pan Jian.

Ground Covered with Brocade see: Pu Di Ji.

Guai Mang Fan Shen Large/monstrous Serpent/Python Turns Over. A Taijiquan move.

Guan to look after or to care about.

Guan see: Kwoon.

Guan Qi Guan literally means "to go through". In Qi Gong training Guan Qi means leading Qi from one place to another.

Guan Sheng Ti Dao Shang Ba Qiao General Guan carries his glaive to Ba Bridge or General Guan Carries Broadsword. A Taijiquan move.

Guan Xi to inspect or look at the breath, meaning to feel/sense the breathing.

Guan Xiang Fa the Behold and Think Method. A Buddhist meditation method.

Guan Xin to inspect or look at Xin.

Gui Ghost.

Gui Qi see: Si Qi.

Gui Xi literally "turtle breathing", meaning skin breathing.

Gun a long Chinese staff weapon.

Guo Bian Pao Wrapping Fire Crackers. A Taijiquan move.

Guo Fen (also Song Ting or Guo Song Ting) one of the primary disciples of Wu Quanyou.

Guolin Qi Gong a Qi Gong form specifically helpful for cancer patients. Also called Walking Qi Gong.

Guoshu literally "national technique". See also: Wushu.

Gu Shu Pan Gen Ancient Tree entwines its Roots. A Taijiquan move.

Gu Qi see: Shi Qi.

Gushing Spring see: Yong Quan.

Gu Sui Bone Marrow.

H

Ha one of the two sounds used in Taijiquan and other Chinese martial styles. The Ha is usually an out breath. See also: Hen.

Hai Di Lao Yue Scoop up the Moon from the Seabottom/ Seabed or Fishing the Moon out from the Bottom of the Sea. A Taijiquan move. Also used as an idiom for a hopeless illusion.

Hai Di Zhen Needle at Sea Bottom. A Taijiquan move.

Halberd see: Ji.

Hand see: Shou.

Hand conceals arm and fist see: Yan Shou Gong Quan.

Hand holds up a thousand kilograms see: Tuo Qian Jin.

Hand supports one thousand pounds see: Tuo Qian Jin.

Han dynasty (206 BC-221 AD) a dynasty in Chinese history.

Han Xiong Ba Bei Sink/hollow Chest and Raise Back.

Hao Style a Taijiquan style created by Hao Weizhen.

Hao Weizhen (1842-1920) created Taijiquan Hao style, student of Li Yi-Yu. One of Hao's most well-known students is Sun Lutang.

Hard Gongfu see: Ying Gong.

Hard Jin see: Ying Jin.

Hard Qi Gong see: Ying Gong.

He close, join, unite, together, harmony, peace.

Head strike Cannon Fists see: Dang Tou Pao.

Health Qi Gong see: Jian Kang Qi Gong.

Heart Yin organ associated with the element Fire. Short form Ht for Heart meridian.

Heaven Tian. Earth (Di), Heaven (Tian) and Man (Ren) are the "Three (Natural) Powers" (San Cai).

Heavenly Circle see: Da Zhou Tian.

Hebei a province in Northern China.

Hebei Xingyi a branch of Xingyi.

He Bu on site, closed step within Tui Shou practice.

Hei Hu Sou Shan Black Tiger searches in the Mountains. A Taijiquan move.

Hei Xiong Fan Shen Black Bear rolls over its back or Black Bear Turns Backward. A Taijiquan move.

Heel Kick see: Deng Jiao or Deng Yi Gen.

He Gu (also Hu Kou) acupuncture point 4 on the Large Intestine meridian (LI-4), translated as Tiger's Mouth. It is located between the index finger and the thumb of the hand.

Hen one of the two sounds used in Taijiquan and other Chinese martial styles. The Hen sound is usually made on an in breath. See also: Ha.

Henan a province in central China.

Heng Jin horizontal energy.

Heshi Hands Prayer Hands. Palms together in front of the breast/sternum.

He Shou Close Hands, Closing Hands.

He Tai Ji Conclude Taiji. A Taijiquan move.

Hidden Thrust Punch see: Yan Shou Gong Quan.

High Pat on Horse see: Gao Tan Ma.

Hit medicine see: Die Da.

Hitting with Elbow see: Shun Lan Zhou.

Holding Coat at the Waist see: Lan Zha Yi.

Hollow Chest and Raise Back see: Han Xiong Ba Bei.

Homage to the Sun see: Chao Yang Tian.

Hook Hand see: Gou Shou.

Horse Riding Stance see: Ma Bu.

Horse Stance see: Ma Bu.

Hou back, behind, after.

Hou Bu moving step within Tui Shou practice.

Hou Tian Fa Post-Heaven Technique.

Hou Tian Qi Post-Birth Qi or Acquired Essence. Qi converted from the air, food, and fluid.

Hou Tui see: Tui Bu.

Hou Zhao Cover the Back or Backward Trick. A Taijiquan move.

Hsin see: Xin.

Hsing Yi Chuan see: Xingyiquan.

Hu Tiger.

Hua slippery. See also: Ba Chu.

Huai Zhong Bao Yue Embracing the Moon. A Taijiquan move.

Hua Jiao Bu Flower or Patterned steps within Tui Shou practice.

Huan slow, relaxed.

Huang Di Yellow Emperor (ca. 2697-2597 BC) Mystical emperor of China who co-authored the book Huang Di Nei Jing Su Wen.

Huang Di Bashiyi Nanjing The Huang Emperor's Canon of Eighty-One Difficult Issues, also referred to as Nan Jing or Classic of Disorders. One of the classics of Traditional Chinese Medicine. The 81 chapters clarify the statements made in the Huang Di Nei Jing Su Wen.

Huang Di Nei Jing Su Wen Yellow Emperor's Classic of Internal Medicine. This ancient medical text is the basis of Traditional Chinese Medicine. It was written by Huang Di, among others.

Huang Long San Jiao Shui Yellow Dragon Stirs the Water Three Times. A Taijiquan move.

Huang Ting literally "yellow hall", meaning the place in which Taoists (in yellow robes) meditate together.

Huan Jing Bu Nao literally "to return the Essence to nourish the brain".

Huan Tiao acupuncture point 30 on the Gallbladder meridian (Gb-30), translated as Jumping Round. It maintains the Qi connection between legs and torso.

Hua Tuo (ca. 140-208) a Chinese doctor who is recorded as the first person in China to use anesthesia during surgery.

Hu Bu Gong Tiger Step Gong. A Qi Gong form.

Hui Gong Exploring Wisdom Qi Gong. A Qi Gong form.

Hui Tou Dang Men Pao Turning Around Forearm Punches. A Taijiquan move.

Hui Tou Jin Gang Dao Dui Varja turns around and pestles. A Taijiquan move.

Hui Tou Jing Lan Zhi Ru Turning Around and Double Forward Elbows. A Taijiquan move.

Hui Yin acupuncture point 1 on the Conception vessel (Cv-1), translated as Meeting of Yin.

Hu Kou see He Gu.

Hu Lei Jia Thunder style Taijiquan.

Hun a type of soul in Chinese philosophy and traditional religion. Hun is believed to be the spiritual, ethereal, Yang soul which leaves the body after death. See also: Po.

Hungry Tiger attacks for Food see: E Hu Pu Shi.

Hungry Tiger Pouncing on its Prey see: E Hu Pu Shi.

Hun Yuan round smoothness. A Zhan Zhuang method.

Hunyuan Palace a name used for the Middle Dantian (Zhong Dantian).

Huo Fire. One of the Five Elements (Wu Xing). Associated with the organs Heart, Small Intestines, Pericardium, and Triple Warmer.

Huo Bu Tui Shou a type of push hands, meaning active-step push hands.

Huo Bu Lan Zha Yi Active Tuck in the Robes. A Taijiquan move.

Huo Long Gong Fire Dragon Gong. A Qi Gong form said to be created by the Taiyang martial stylists.

Huo Lu Fire Path. A meditation method.

Huo Qi Fire Qi. Huo Qi is "vital Qi" in a being as opposed to "dead Qi" (Si Qi).

Hu Xi Jian Protect the Knee. A Taijiquan move.

Hu Xin Dao Sabre Protects the Heart or Shielding the Heart with the Sabre. A Taijiquan move.

Hu Xing Quan Protect the Heart Punch or protect the heart with both fists. A Taijiquan move.

Hu Yuan literally "completely round" or "round smoothness". A variation of Zhan Zhuang.

I

I see: Yi.

I Ching see: Yi Jing.

I Chuan see: Yiquan.

Inclined Posture see: Xie Xing.

I Ging see: Yi Jing.

Immortal One Seizes Once see: Shen Xian Yi Ba Zhua.

Immortal Points the Way see: Xian Ren Zhi Lu.

Inherited Essence see: Prenatal Essence.

Insubstantial Stance see: Xu Bu.

Intent see: Yi.

Internal Kidneys see: Nei Shen.

Internal Martial Arts see Nei Jia.

Ip Tai Tak (1929-2004) one of the three disciples of Yang style Taijiquan master Yang Shou Chung.

Iron Palm see: Ying Gong or Tie Zhang.

Iron Shirt see: Tie Shan and Jin Zhong Zhao.

J

Jade Maiden Shuttles back and forth see: Yu Nü Chuan Suo.

Jade Pillow see: Yu Zhen.

Jen Mai see: Ren Mai.

Ji press or squeeze. One of the eight basic methods of Taijiquan (Ba Men). Part of Grasp Sparrow's Tail (Lan Que Wei).

Ji halberd. A long handled weapon with pointed tip and crescent blade.

Jia family or school. Also used as "frame" to describe the differences in appearance, especially in Chen style Taijiquan forms. See Da Jia, Lao Jia, Xin Xia, Xiao Jia.

Jia Guan The False Look. A meditation method.

Jia Gu Wen Oracle Bone Script. Earliest known form of Chinese writing in the late 2nd millennium BC. Bones as well as turtle shells were used, thus sometimes called Shell and Bone Script.

Jian straight sword.

Jian strong, solid, unyielding.

Jiang Fa (1574-1655) a Zhaobao style Taijiquan master.

Jiang Kang Qi Gong Health Qi Gong. Qi Gong forms which mainly focuses on improved health. See: types of Qi Gong.

Jian Jing acupuncture point 21 on the Gallbladder meridian (Gb-21), translated as Shoulder Well.

Jiao Hua Gong Beggar Gong. A Qi Gong form.

Jiao Lian instructor, trainer, coach.

Ji Ben Ba Shi the eight fundamental stances practiced in Taijiquan.

Ji Ben Gong (Fu) general foundation exercises in Chinese martial arts.

Ji Di Chui Punch towards the Ground. A Taijiquan move.

Jiexi acupuncture point 41 on the Stomach meridian (St-41), translated as Ravine Divine.

Jimen acupuncture point 11 on the Stomach meridian (St-11), translated as Winnower Gate.

Jin (also: Chin) integrated strength/sensitivity, kinetic energy, power, internal force. Taijiquan (and other internal martial arts) aim to development Jin instead of Li (muscular strength) or Zhuo Li (crude strength). Generally, a high level of Jin means more Qi and less Li is used. Different types of Jin are sensing Jin, neutralizing Jin or emitting Jin.

Jin Metal. One of the Five Elements (Wu Xing). Associated with Lungs and Large Intestines.

Jin Bu Step Forward with the front foot. Also named Qianjing. One of the five basic steps (Wu Bu).

Jin Dan Golden Elixir.

Jin Dian sometimes translated as "energy points".

Jin dynasty (1115-1234) a dynasty in Chinese history.

Jing Essence. It is the most dense physical matter (as opposed to Shen and Qi) and stored in the Kidneys. Essence, Qi, and Shen are considered the Three Treasures (San Bao).

Jing see: Meridian.

Jing calm, quiet.

Jin Gang Gong Diamond Qi Gong. A Qi Gong form.

Jin Gang Zhi Steel Finger or One Finger Method. A Qi Gong training method. See also Yi Zhi Chan.

Jing Gang Dao Dui Buddha's Warrior Attendant Pounds Mortar. A Taijiquan move.

Jing Gong meditative/passive/tranquil Qi Gong. Qi Gong that is usually practiced while maintaining one body posture. Opposite is Dong Gong.

Jing Lian to refine/purify a substance or one's skills.

Jing Liang excellent or of superior quality.

Jing Luo the meridian system or channel network in Traditional Chinese Medicine.

Jing Mai see: Shi Er Jing.

Jingmen acupuncture point 25 on the Gallbladder meridian (Gb-25), translated as Capital Gate or Essence Doors.

Jin Gong a training method to gain maximum Jin.

Jing Qi Essence Qi. Qi that has been converted from Jing.

Jing Shen spirit, mind consciousness; vigor, vitality, drive, spiritual.

Jing Shen Qi Gong Spiritual Qi Gong. Qi Gong exercises which are practiced to achieve harmony, self-awareness and spiritual enlightenment. See also: types of Qi Gong.

Jin Gung Dao Dui Strong Man Pounds the Mortar. A Taijiquan move.

Jing Xi literally "clean breathing". Used as "regulated breathing", indicating "to use natural breathing to regulate thoughts".

Jing Zi literally "essence child", meaning sperm.

Jin Ji Du Li Golden Rooster/Cock stands on one Leg. A Taijiquan move.

Jin Kui Yao Kue "Essential Prescriptions from the Golden Cabinet". A Chinese clinical book which discusses the use of breathing and acupuncture to maintain good Qi flow. Written by Zhang Zhong-Jing (150-219).

Jin Ye a term in Traditional Chinese Medicine for bodily fluids or moisture. Anything that cannot be classified as Qi or Blood, e.g. cerebrospinal fluid, synovial fluids, interstitial fluids, sweat, mucus, tears, saliva, sexual secretions, urine.

Jin Zhong Zhao Golden Bell Cover. A hard Gongfu training to strengthen the outside (muscles, bones, sinews) and inside (the inner organs). Similar to Tie Shan.

Jiu nine (9).

Jiuwei acupuncture point 15 on the Conception Vessel (Cv-15), translated as Turtledove Tail.

Juan Lian Dao Tui Nan Zhe Bi waving the curtain – stepping back – the enemy cannot find an opportunity. A Taijiquan move.

Ju Dao Mo Qi Huai Bao Yue raise blade as if waving a banner and embracing the moon. A Taijiquan move.

Jueyin absolute Yin.

Ju Jing Hui Shen literally "gathering Jing to meet Shen", meaning to concentrate one's attention.

Jump see: Tiao.

Jung Mai see: Zhong Mai.

K

Kai to open.

Kai Bu Sidestep.

Kai Li Bu Open Stance/Step.

Kaimen Chinese Taoist Yoga.

Kai Shou open hands, opening hands.

Kan one of the Eight Trigrams. See: Bagua.

Kao (shoulder) strike, bump. One of the eight basic methods of Taijiquan (Ba Men).

Khou see: Kao.

Ki Japanese for Qi.

Kick Foot see: Fen Jiao.

Kick with heel see: Deng Yi Gen.

Kidneys Yin organ associated with the element Water. Short form Ki for Kidney meridian.

Kong Guan The Empty Look. A meditation method.

Kong Kong Dang Dang absolutely empty (space), complete vacuum.

Kong Ming (also Kung Ming or Zhuge Liang) (181-234) a statesman during the Three Kingdoms Period. Recognized as an accomplished strategist, he has been compared to Sun Tzu, author of The Art of War.

Kong Qi air, atmosphere.

Kou Bu Buckle Step or Toe-in-step.

Kowtow see: Bai Shi.

Ku see: Zuo Gu.

Kua (also Kwa) direct translation: groin, crotch, hip. Kua refers to the area around the hip-crease (inguinal crease), the natural fold which stretches up diagonally. From Huiyin it runs on each side of the body along the inguinal ligament through the inside of the pelvis to the top of the hip bones.

Kun one of the Eight Trigrams. See: Bagua.

Kung see: Gong.

Kung Fu see Gongfu.

Kuoshou see: Guoshu.

Kwa see: Kua.

Kwoon a training hall for Chinese martial arts, also called Guan. Better known by the Japanese term Dojo.

L

Lama title for a spiritual teacher in Tibetan Buddhism.

Lan to block somebody's path, to parry.

Lan Que Wei Grasp Sparrow's Tail. A series of four basic Taijiquan postures: Peng, Lu, Ji, An.

Lan Shi Mi Cang "Secret Library of the Orchid Room". A Chinese medical and Qi Gong book written by Li Guo around 960-1368.

Lan Zha Yi Holding Coat at the Waist or Lazy about tying the Coat. A Taijiquan move.

Lao Gong acupuncture point 8 on the Pericardium meridian (Pc-8), translated as Palace of Toil or Work palace. It is located in the center of the palm. It is an important point to sense or send Qi.

Lao Jia old frame. Overarching name for two Chen style Taijiquan forms: Yi Lu and Er Lu.

Lao Shi see: Qi Gong master.

Lao-Tzu see: Laozi.

Laozi (also Lao-Tzu). Literally Master Lao. Legendary figure usually dated to around the 6th century BC. Author of the Tao Te Ching.

Large Frame see: Da Jia.

Large Intestines Yang organ associated with the element Metal. Short form LI for Large Intestines meridian.

Large Serpent Turns Over see: Guai Mang Fan Shen.

Lazy about tying the Coat see: Lan Zha Yi.

Lean with Back see: Bei Zhe Kao.

Lee style Taijiquan a style of Taijiquan brought to the West by Chan Kam Lee.

Left Zou.

Legacy see: Lineage.

Legs Sweeping see: Sao Tang Tui.

Leng cold. See also: Ba Chu.

Li (muscular) power, strength, force. See also: Jin.

Li one of the Eight Trigrams. See: Bagua.

Lian to practice, train, drill, exercise, perfect one's skill.

Lian Dan "to concoct pills of immortality", meaning alchemy. Chinese alchemy distinguishes Nei Dan (internal alchemy) and Wei Dan (external alchemy).

Liang cool. See also: Ba Chu.

Liang Dynasty (502-587) a dynasty in Chinese history.

Liang Jing Hua Qi literally "to refine Essence and transform it into Qi".

Liang Yi two Primordial Powers, usually Heaven & Earth or Yin & Yang.

Lian Qi literally "to practice/exercise Qi".

Lian Qi Hua Shen to practice transforming Qi to Shen.

Lian Shen to train Shen.

Lian Shen Fa Xu literally "to refine Shen into emptiness". A term in Taoist Qi Gong training.

Lian Shen Liao Xing literally "to refine Shen and end

human nature". A term in spiritual Qi Gong training.

Lie (also Lieh) to split, break open. One of the eight basic methods of Taijiquan (Ba Men).

Lift Hands see: Ti Shou.

Li Guo author of the book Lan Shi Mi Cang.

Lineage in martial arts it means an uninterrupted line of masters and worthy students, who pass on the knowledge to the next generation. Ideally, a lineage can be traced back to the creator of a specific martial art or style.

Lineage disciple see: Di Zi.

Ling quick, alert.

Ling zero (0).

Ling spirit, soul, spiritual world. Often used together with Shen (Ling Shen) or Qi (Ling Qi).

Ling Bao Bi Fa "Spiritual Treasure to Reach the End Method". A text about Qi Gong methods.

Ling Dong to be quick-witted, also used as "subtle movement".

Linghuo flexible, agile.

Ling Qi supernatural energy, power, force.

Ling Shen supernatural/divine spirit.

Ling Shu a part of the medical classic Huang Di Nei Jing Su Wen that discusses acupuncture therapy.

Ling Tai acupuncture point 10 on the Governing vessel (Gv-10), translated as Spirit Tower.

Ling Zhi literally "spirit mushroom", also called reishi mushroom. A hard, dark brownish fungus which is used in

Traditional Chinese Medicine for its supporting effects on the immune system.

Lin Hou Sheng (born in 1939) creator of Shibashi Qi Gong.

Linking Vessel see: Yin Wei Mai or Yang Wei Mai.

Li Qi see: Qi Li.

Li Shi Zhen (1518-1593) a Chinese doctor, author of a book about the eight Qi vessels, Qi Jing Ba Mai Kao.

Listening Hands see: Tui Shou.

Listening power see: Ting Jin.

Liu six (6).

Liu Feng Si Bi Six Sealing and Four Closing. A Taijiquan move.

Liu Han Wen (1921-2004) creator of Chan Mi Gong.

Liu He Ba Fa Quan Literally "Six Harmonies Eight Methods Boxing". An internal Chinese martial art. The Taoist sage Chen Po is often credited as the creator of Liu He Ba Fa Quan.

Liu Zi Jue Six Healing Sounds Qi Gong. A Qi Gong form involving the coordination of movement and breathing patterns with specific sounds (xu, he, hu, si, chui, xi).

Liver Yin organ associated with the element Wood. Short form Li for Liver meridian.

Lo, Benjamin Pang Jeng (Ben Lo, born 1927) a Taijiquan master, student of Cheng Manching.

Long Chinese Dragon. Legendary creatures in Chinese mythology and folklore. They traditionally symbolize potent and auspicious powers, particularly control over water. The dragon is also a symbol of power, strength, and good luck.

Long bow stance see: Yu Gong Bu.

Long Form see: 108 form.

Lotus kick see: Bai Lian.

Lou Xi (also Chu Shou) Gathering at the Knees or Brush Knee. A Taijiquan move.

Lou Xi Ao Bu Brush Knee and Step Forward. A Taijiquan move.

Lou Zai Huai Zhong You Bao Yue Blade falls into Chest as you embrace the Moon. A Taijiquan move.

Lower Burner see: Xiao Jiao.

Lower Dantian see: Xia Dantian.

Lower Stance in Front of Chamber and Twist Step see: Qian Tang Ao Bu.

Lu/Lü Rollback or absorbing. A technique for leading the opponent's attack past oneself. One of the moves within the Grasp the Sparrow's Tail sequence (Lan Que Wei) and one of the eight basic methods of Taijiquan (Ba Men).

Luan Cai Hua Tui Shou with free flowing steps.

Lungs Yin organ associated with the element Metal. Short form Lu for Lung meridian.

Luo see: Jing Luo.

Luohan (also Arahat) someone who has attained nirvana or is far advanced along the path of enlightenment.

Luohan Shou Luohan Hands. A Qi Gong form originated from the Shaolin monastery.

Luohan Xiang Long Luohan Defeats/Tames the Dragon. A Taijiquan move.

Luo Hua Shi Falling Flowers. A Taijiquan move.

M

Ma Bu Horse Stance or Horse-Riding Stance. An important posture in Asian martial arts.

Mai see: Meridian.

Man (person) Ren. Earth (Di), Heaven (Tian) and Man (Ren) are the "Three (Natural) Powers" (San Cai).

Mao Bu Cat Stance.

Marrow Cleansing see: Xi Sui Jing.

Martial Arts see: Wushu.

Martial Arts Qi Gong see: Wushu Qi Gong.

Martial flower see: Wu Hua.

Mawangdui Daoyin Qi Gong from the Mawangdui Silk Paintings. A Qi Gong form.

Ma Yueliang (1901-1998) a Wu style Taijiquan master. Married to Wu Quanyou's granddaughter Wu Ying-Hua.

Medical Qi Gong see: Yi Liao Qi Gong.

Meditation a practice where an individual trains the mind. Usually involves experiencing moments of inner stillness. Taijiquan is sometimes referred to as "meditation in motion".

Meditative Qi Gong see: Jing Gong.

Mencius (372-289BC, also Mengzi) a Chinese philosopher who followed the philosophy of Confucius.

Men Ren literally "door person". Someone who has become a disciple of a master.

Merging Step see: Bing Bu.

Meridians paths through which Qi circulates around the body (also called channels, vessels, Jing, Mai). The most important meridian networks are Shi Er Jing (Jing Mai, 12 main meridians) and Qi Jing Ba Mai (Eight Extraordinary Meridians).

Meridian clock see: Zi Wu Liu Zhu.

Metal see: Jin.

Mian soft, continuous, also means cotton.

Mian Quan Cotton Fist or Cotton Boxing. A name sometimes used for Taijiquan. See also: Gang Bao Mian Hua.

Middle Burner see: Zhong Jiao.

Middle Dantian see: Zhong Dantian.

Middle Tray see: Zhong Pan.

Ming life, fate.

Ming dynasty (1368-1644) a dynasty in Chinese history.

Ming Men acupuncture point 4 on the Governing Channel (Gv-4), translated as Life Gate. It is located approximately opposite the navel.

Ming Tian Gu beating the heavenly drum or sound the heavenly drum. A Qi Gong exercise where the back of the head is hit by the fingers to clear the mind and wake up.

Misplace the bones see: Cuo Cu.

Mi Zong Vajrayana or Tantric Buddhism.

Mo to wipe. Sometimes used for hand or arm motions.

Moisture see: Jin Ye.

Mo Mei Gong Wipe the brow palms. A Taijiquan move.

Monstrous Serpent Turns Over see: Guai Mang Fan Shen.

Mo Pan Jian Grinding Disk Sword. A Taijiquan move.

Mo Tzu see: Mozi.

Moving meditation meditation (including relaxing, stilling the mind etc) done while continuously moving. Taijiquan is sometimes referred to as "meditation in motion".

Moving Qi Gong see: Dong Gong.

Moxibustion a traditional Chinese medicine therapy which consists of burning dried mugwort (moxa) on particular points on the body.

Mozi (ca. 468-ca. 391BC) a Chinese philosopher.

Mo Yao Dao Hui Tou Pan Gen Circling the Hip "like a Millstone" - Turning the Head – Winding the Roots. Also called Waist-level blade grinds around coiled roots. A Taijiquan move.

Mu Wood. One of the Five Elements (Wu Xing). Associated with Liver and Gallbladder.

Mudra a symbolic or ritual hand/finger/body position. It can be used to stimulate different parts of the body and mind.

Muscle/Tendon Change Qi Gong see: Yi Jin Jing.

N

Na Fa locking and grappling.

Nanjing Central Guoshu Institute see: Central Guoshu Institute.

Nan Jing see: Huang Di Bashiyi Nanjing.

Nao Sui brain.

Natural Breathing see: Shun Hu Xi.

Naturalism a Taoist concept that happiness and longevity are achieved by following the soft, yielding, and changing ways of nature.

Navel see: Duqi.

Na Zha explores the Sea see: Na Zha Tan Hai.

Na Zha Tan Hai Na Zha explores the Sea. A Taijiquan move.

Needle at Sea Bottom see: Hai Di Zhen.

Nei Dan Internal Alchemy. Within Chinese alchemy the creation of an elixir inside the body with the help of physical, mental, and spiritual practices. The aim is to prolong life and to create an immortal spiritual body. Qi Gong and meditation are important parts of Nei Dan. See also: Lian Dan.

Nei Gong literally "Inner Work". Chinese breathing, meditation, and spiritual practice methods associated with Daoism and Chinese martial arts. Qi Gong is a form of non-martial Nei Gong. Taijiquan is an example of martial Nei Gong.

Nei Gong Tu Shuo "Illustrated Explanation of Nei Gong". Name of a Qi Gong book edited by Wang Zu-Yuan in 1881.

Nei Jia literally "Internal Family", meaning internal martial arts (also Neiquan), which focus on Nei Gong and often include Qi Gong practice. The most known are Taijiquan, Xingyiquan, Baguazhang, and Liu He Ba Fa. The external martial arts are known as Wai Jia.

Nei Jin literally "Internal Power".

Nei Jing see: Huang Di Nei Jing Su Wen.

Nei Jin Li similar to Nei Jin, but emphasizing that even with internal power, one must use the muscles to some degree.

Neiquan see: Neijia.

Nei San He three inner harmonies, meaning Yi, Qi and Shen should be united.

Nei Shen literally "Internal Kidneys". The organs Kidneys are called Nei Shen in Traditional Chinese Medicine. See also: Wai Shen.

Nei Shi Fan Ting literally "to look and listen inwardly" during meditation.

Nei Shi Gongfu literally "the art of looking internally".

New Frame see: Xin Jia.

Nian to stick, to adhere.

Ni Hu Xi Reverse Breathing, also called Paradoxical/ Oppositional Breathing, Fan Fu Hu Xi, Fan Hu Xi or Daoist breathing. A breathing technique where the stomach contracts during inhalation and expands during exhalation. As it can induce hypertension and anxiety, it should only be practiced under supervision.

Nine jiu (9).

Ning Shen literally "to concentrate" or "focus the spirit".

Ni Wan Gong Mud Ball Palace. Alternative name for Bai Hui.

Nod the Head see: Dian Tou.

Nuan warm. See also: Ba Chu.

Nutritive Qi see: Ying Qi.

O

Oblique posture see: Xie Xing.

Offer Wine – Pick up Cloak – Suddenly Turning Back see: Di Jiu Tiao Pao Meng Hui Tou.

Old Frame see: Lao Jia.

One (1) yi.

One Finger Method see: Jin Gang Zhi.

One Finger Zen see: Yi Zhi Chan.

Open Push Hands Push Hands with free structure.

Opening hands see: Kai Shou.

Open Stance/Step see: Kai Li Bu.

Oppositional Breathing see: Ni Hu Xi.

Oracle bone script see: Jia Gu Wen.

Organ see: Zang Fu.

Organ (Networks) see: Zang Fu.

Original Essence see: Yuan Jing.

Original Qi see: Yuan Qi.

Original Shen see: Yuan Shen.

Over-Training see: San Gong.

Overturning Flowers and Waving Sleeves see: Fan Hua Wu Xiou.

P

Pai clique/school/group of thought or boxing.

Pai Bu see: Bai Bu.

Pa Kua see: Bagua.

Pan see: ban.

Pan to look. See also: You Pan.

Pan Gu Shengong Pan Gu Mystical Qi Gong. A Qi Gong set.

Pan Lan Chui see: Ban Lan Chui.

Pao Chui see: Er Lu.

Paradoxical Breathing see: Ni Hu Xi.

Parry Lan (as in Ban Lan Chui).

Parting the grass looking for snakes see: Bo Cao Xun She.

Part the Wild Horse's Mane see: Ye Ma Fen Zong.

Passive Qi Gong see: Jing Gong.

Pathogenic Factors see: Six Excesses.

Pat Horse on High Back see: Gao Tan Ma.

Patterned Steps see: Hua Jiao Bu.

Penetrating Vessel see: Chong Mai.

Peng Ward-off. One of the primary postures of the Grasp the Sparrow's Tail sequence (Lan Que Wei) and one of the eight basic methods of Taijiquan (Ba Men).

Peng Jin expansive energy.

Pengju see: Yue Fei.

Pericardium Yin function which is associated with the element Fire, also called "heart protector". Pericardium, like the Triple Burner (San Jiao) is not associated with an anatomical entity. Short form Pc for Pericardium meridian.

Phoenix nods its Head see: Feng Huang Dian Tou.

Pie literally "to cast away or to throw". Also used for pivoting of a foot on the heel.

Pie Shen Chui (also Bi Shen Chui) Chop with Fist or Shield body bunch or Flinging Body Punch. A Taijiquan move.

Pie Shen Quan Rotational Body Punch. A Taijiquan move.

Pi Jia Zi Wearing the Frame. A Taijiquan move.

Pinyin the official romanization system for Standard Chinese. It was approved in 1958 by the Chinese government. In Pinyin it is Qi Gong and Taijiquan, in Wade-Giles Ch'i Kung and T'ai Chi Ch'üan.

Pipa a Chinese instrument similar to a lute or guitar.

Pi Shen Chui see: Pie Shen Quan.

Pi Shen Fu Hu Diagonal Subdue Tiger or Attack the Tiger. A Taijiquan move.

Play the Pipa see: Shouhui Pipa.

Ploughing the grass and searching for a snake see: Bo Cao Xun She.

Pluck see: Cai.

Pluck the stars and rotate the constellations see: Zhai Xing Huan Dao.

Po a type of soul in Chinese philosophy and traditional religion. Po is believed to be the corporeal, substantive, Yin soul, which remains with the corpse after death. See also: Hun.

Pointing to the Crotch see: Zhi Dang Chui.

Pole Standing see: Zhan Zhuang.

Pose like a Hero see: Cheng Ying Hao.

Pose with a raised blade see: Shi Zi Yi Dao Wang Ju Qi.

Post-birth Qi see: Hou Tian Qi.

Post-Heaven Technique see: Hou Tian Fa.

Postnatal Essence see: Hou Tian Qi.

Posture see: Ding Dian.

Posture holding see: Ding Shi.

Prayer Hands see: Heshi Hands.

Prenatal Essence see: Xian Tian Qi.

Preparation see: Yu Bei Shi or Qi Shi.

Press see: Ji.

Primary Channels see: Shi Er Jing.

Primordial Qi Gong see: Wuji Qi Gong.

Protective Qi see: Wei Qi.

Protect the Heart Punch/Fist see: Hu Xing Quan.

Protect the Knee see: Hu Xi Jian.

Pu Bu Flat Stance or Drop Stance.

Pu Di Ji Ground Covered with Brocade. A Taijiquan move.

Pull the Grass in search of the Snake see: Bo Cao Xun She.

Punch Chui.

Punch Down see: Zai Chui.

Punch Downward see: Wo Di Pao.

Punching from Bottom to Top see: Wo Di Da Zhuo Pao.

Punch of Draping over Body see: Pi Shen Chui.

Punch to the Groin see: Zhi Dang Chui.

Punch towards the Ground see: Ji Di Chui.

Push see: An.

Push Hands see: Tui Shou.

Push with Both Hands see: Shuang Tui Shou.

Pu Tiu Pu Ting see: Chan Lien Tieh Sui Pu Tiu Pu Ting.

Q

Qi gas, air, smell, breath, vital energy. Meaning the "energy" which circulates in all living entities. Qi is an invisible substance and immaterial force but can show in manifestations. Known as Ki in Japan.
The traditional Chinese character for Qi consists of one part representing "vapor or steam" and one part meaning "rice". It is said that it symbolizes distilled essence, like steam that rises from a pot of cooking rice.

Qi seven (7).

Qian thousand (1000).

Qian one of the Eight Trigrams. See: Bagua.

Qiang spear, lance (weapon).

Qiang Shen to strengthen one's body, to build up one's health (through exercise, nutrition etc.).

Qian Jin Yi Fang "Supplement to the Formulas of a Thousand Gold Worth", also called Thousand Gold Prescriptions. A medical book written by the doctor Sun Simiao (died in 682). It lists 2000 recipes for medicines and health exercises.

Qianjing see: Jin Bu or Chin.

Qian Jin Zhui literally "to drop thousand pounds", meaning Thousand Pound Sinking. A training method in Chinese martial arts where the practitioner imagines rooting into the ground as if weighing a thousand pounds.

Qian Tang Ao Bu Lower Stance in Front of Chamber and Twist step, also called Wade Forward and Twist Step. A Taijiquan move.

Qian Zhao Forward Trick or Cover the Front. A Taijiquan move.

Qiao Mai Heel Vessel. see Yin Qiao Mai or Yang Qiao Mai.

Qi Chong acupuncture point 30 on the Stomach meridian (St-30), translated as Surging Qi.

Qie Di Long see: Que Di Long.

Qi Gong literally "Qi work" or "life energy cultivation". The art and science to cultivate and balance Qi, deeply rooted in Chinese medicine, philosophy, and martial arts. It is a system of coordinated body postures, moves, breathing, and meditation techniques to improve health, to calm the mind, and to condition for martial arts. Sometimes also called Daoyin, Nei Gong, Yang Sheng, Xing Qi or Tu Gu Na Xin.

Qi Gong An Mo Qi Gong massage.

Qi Gong Deviation see: Zou Huo Ru Mo.

Qi Gong Master also Lao Shi, Shi Fu or Sifu. Lao Shi can also mean professor or teacher. Shifu (meaning teaching father) is a title for a skillful person. It can refer to anyone who has mastered a skill (not necessarily a Qi Gong or martial art skill).

Qi Gong Meditation see: Jing Gong.

Qi Gong Psychosis see: Zou Huo Ru Mo.

Qi Hai acupuncture point 6 on the Conception channel (Cv-6), translated as Sea of Qi. This point is critical for the development of Qi. See also: Dantian.

Qi Huo literally "to catch fire". A term in Qi Gong used to describe the time when Qi starts to build up at the Xia Dantian.

Qi Jing Ba Mai literally "Strange Channels Eight Vessels", usually referred to as "Eight Extraordinary Vessels". Not directly associated with organs (Zhang Fu), they are considered to be storage vessels or reservoirs of energy. Their names are Ren Mai, Du Mai, Chong Mai, Dai Mai, Yin Wei Mai, Yang Wei Mai, Yin Qiao Mai, and Yang Qiao Mai.

Qi Jing Ba Mai Kao "Deep Study of the Extraordinary Eight Vessels". A book about the Eight Extraordinary Channels written by Li Shi Zhen (1518-1593).

Qi Li (or Li Qi) Muscular Power supported by Qi. Stimulating the muscles through Qi flow, while keeping the muscles relaxed.

Qi Mai Qi vessels. See: meridians.

Qi Men acupuncture point 14 on the Liver meridian (Li-14), translated as Cycle Gate.

Qin dynasty (221BC-206BC) a Chinese dynasty in Chinese history.

Qing light, easy, gentle, soft. See also: Ba Chu.

Qing Dan light food (not greasy or strongly flavored).

Qing dynasty (1644-1912) the last dynasty in Chinese history.

Qing Gong Lightness Skill.

Qing Ling quick and skillful, agile.

Qing Long Bai Wei Blue Dragon Sways its Tail. A Taijiquan move.

Qing Long Chu Shui Green-Blue (Azure) Dragon Emerges from Water. A Taijiquan move.

Qing Long Zhuan Shen Blue Dragon turns over. A Taijiquan move.

Qing Xiu Pai Pure Cultivation Branch. Meaning a school of Daoist Qi Gong training.

Qin Na (also: Chin Na) Seizing the Joints. The set of joint lock techniques used in Chinese martial arts to control or lock an opponent's joints or muscles/tendons so he cannot move. Categories of Qin Na are Fen Jin, Cuo Cu, Bi Qi, and Dian

Xue.

Qin Yuan Zhuo Ma literally "seize the ape and catch the horse". A Qi Gong phrase to describe the practice of regulating the mind.

Qi Qing Liu Yu Seven emotions and six desires. Buddhists believe that all human suffering is caused by them. The seven emotions are pleasure, anger, sorrow, joy, love, hate, and desire. The six desires are associated with the six senses (eyes, ears, nose, tongue, body, and mind).

Qi Se Qi appearance or complexion. It is the impression a Chinese medicine practitioner has of the patient's state of health.

Qi Sensation see: Ba Chu.

Qi Shi preparation, beginning or wake the Qi. A Taijiquan move.

Qi Shi literally "to look at/inspect/observe Qi".

Qi Xi Qi Breath.

Qi Xing Seven Stars. See also: Shang Bu Qi Xing.

Qi Xue literally "Qi Blood".

Quan fist. Also used to name a martial art style, e.g. Taijiquan or Xingyiquan.

Quan Pao Chui The Whole Cannon Fist. A Taijiquan move.

Quan Wu Hua Full Turn or Dance of the Blossom or Full Martial Flower. A Taijiquan move.

Qu Chi acupuncture point 11 on the Large Intestine meridian (LI-11), translated as Pool at the Bend.

Que Di Long (also Qie Di Long) Earthworm burrowing under the mud or Sparrow Dashes Earth Dragon or Dragon hacks the ground. A Taijiquan move.

R

Raise a Lamp toward Heaven see: Chao Tian Deng.

Raise blade as if waving a banner and embracing the moon see: Ju Dao Mo Qi Huai Bao Yue.

Raise glaive and survey the doomed see: Zai Ju Qing Long Kan Sin Ren.

Raise glaive to test the water see: Fan Shen Zai Ju Long Tan Shui.

Raise Hands see: Ti Shou.

Re to warm up; heat. See also: Ba Chu.

Reed, Lou (1942-2013) an American musician, singer and songwriter (e.g. "Walk on the Wild Side"), who was also a Taijiquan practitioner.

Relax see: Fang Song.

Relaxation Qi Gong see: Fang Song Gong.

Ren man or mankind. Earth (Di), Heaven (Tian) and Man (Ren) are the "Three (Natural) Powers" (San Cai).

Ren Mai Conception Channel, also called Jen Mai. It is the primary Yin meridian and corresponds to the mid line traveling up the front of the body from Hui Yin to the tip of the tongue. It is one of the Eight Extraordinary Channels.

Re Qi steam, heat.

Ren Qi human Qi.

Repulse Monkey see: Dao Juan Gong.

Rest Stance Xie Bu.

Retreat to Ride Tiger see: Tui Bu Kua Hu.

Return to Taiji see: Taiji Huan Yuan.

Reverse Breathing see: Ni Hu Xi.

Ride Tiger see: Tui Bu Kua Hu.

Riding Dragon Backwards see: Dao Qi Long.

Right You.

Right hand holds up a thousand kilograms see: You Tuo Qian Jin.

Right Stomp – one Root see: You Deng Yi Gen.

Ri Tao San Huan Sun braces three things. A Taijiquan move.

Rollback see: Lu.

Rolling away from the blade see: Ying Feng Gun Bi.

Rotational Body Punch see: Pie Shen Quan.

Rooting the ability to keep your footing or connection with the ground while experiencing incoming force. The idea is to sink the body energy and root it into the earth.

Rou soft, gentle, yielding.

Ruan soft, flexible. See also: Ba Chu.

Ruan Jin literally "Soft Jin", meaning muscle usage is minimal.

Ruan Ying Jin Soft Hard Jin. A type of Jin where muscles are relaxed and soft until the moment the power reaches the opponent's body – then the physical body tightens to avoid injuries.

Rub with Foot see: Ca Jiao.

Rufeng Shibi Appears Closed or Apparent Closeup. A Taijiquan move.

Rugen acupuncture point 18 on the Stomach meridian (St-18), translated as Breast Root.

Ru Jia literally "Confucian family", meaning Confucianism.

Ru Jing literally "immigration". In the context of meditation it means Entering Tranquility or tranquil meditation. Known in Japanese as Zazen. Also called Zuo Wang.

Ru Men literally "enter the door". It means becoming an "indoor student" of a master. See also: Bai Shi.

Ru Men Shi Shi "The Confucian Point of View". A book written by Zhang Zihe (1156-1228) which describes Qi Gong exercises.

S

Sabre see: Dao.

Sabre Protects the Heart see: Hu Xin Dao.

Sage see: Xian.

San three (3).

San Bao Three Treasures, referring to Jing, Qi, and Shen. They are also called San Yuan or San Ben.

San Ben Three Foundations. See also: San Bao.

San Cai Three Powers. The Three Powers are Heaven (Tian), Earth (Di), and Man (Ren).

San Chin a martial art stance where the front leg is slightly forward and slightly angled inward. The back foot is angled inward with toes pointing at the front foot toes.

Sanda see: Sanshou.

San Gong literally "to disperse achievement", meaning over-training.

San Guang literally "three lights". Can mean the sun, the moon, and the stars. Within Traditional Chinese Medicine, it is said that the Liver shows the Hun light in the eyes, the Lungs show the Po light in the nose, and the Kidneys show the Jing light in the ears.

San Hua Ju Ding Three flowers reach the top or Three Flowers Condensing onto the Head. A Neidan term.

San Huan Zhang Change Palms Three Times. A Taijiquan move.

San Jiao (SJ) Triple Burner or Triple Heater. A bodily function that does not correspond to a specific physical substance (like Pericardium). San Jiao is one of the six Yang channels.

In Traditional Chinese Medicine, the upper body is divided into three areas: Upper Burner (Shang Jiao): chest, including heart and lungs; Middle Burner (Zhong Jiao): solar plexus to navel, including stomach and spleen; Lower Burner (Xiao Jiao): lower abdomen, including kidneys and liver.

San Shi Qi Shi literally "Thirty-Seven Postures". Said to be one of the earlier forms of Taijiquan.

Sanshou free sparring, also called Sanda or Chinese boxing.

Santi Shi Trinity Pole Standing. A Zhan Zhuang variation.

San Yuan Three Origins. See also: San Bao.

Sao Tang Tui Sweeping Legs. A Taijiquan move.

Scatter the Clouds and See the Sun see: Bo Yun Wang Ri.

Scoop up the Moon from the Bottom of the Sea see: Hai Di Lao Yue.

Screen hand and punch see: Yan Shou Chui.

Se harsh. See also: Ba Chu.

Seal the Breath see: Bi Qi.

Seating the wrist see: Zuo Wan.

Second Form see: Er Lu.

Sensing Hands see: Tui Shou.

Separation Kick see: Fen Jiao.

Separate Foot see: Fen Jiao.

Separate the muscles see: Fen Jin.

Separate the Weed on the side to search for the Snake

see Bo Cao Xun She.

Settle down wrist see: Zuo Wan.

Seven qi (7).

Seven Stars see: Qi Xing.

Shake foot and Stretch Down see: Die Cha.

Shaking power see: Dou Jin.

Shaman see: Wu.

Shan to avoid, to dodge.

Shang upper, above.

Shang Bu step forward with the back foot.

Shang Bu Qi Xing Step forward to the Seven Stars. A Taijiquan move.

Shang Dantian Upper Dantian, located between the eyebrows or the third eye. Associated with Shen. Also called Shenji Palace.

Shang dynasty (ca.1600BC-1046BC) a dynasty in Chinese history.

Shang Huo literally "excessive internal heat".

Shang Jiao Upper Burner. One of the Triple Burners (San Jiao) in Traditional Chinese Medicine. It is located in the chest between the throat and solar plexus.

Shang San Bu Three Steps Forward. A Taijiquan move.

Shang San Dao Xia Sha Xu Chu Three Fierce Steps forward to frighten Xu Chu or Three Upward Movements. A Taijiquan move.

Shang Xia Xie Ci Thrust Slantwise up and down. A Taijiquan move.

Shan Tong Bei Fan Penetrates Back, also Turn Back Quickly, Fan Through Back or Flash the Back. A Taijiquan move.

Shan Zhong acupuncture point 17 on the Conception meridian (Cv-17), translated as Chest Center.

Shanzi fan (weapon).

Shaohai acupuncture point 3 on the Heart meridian (Ht-3), translated as Lesser Sea.

Shaolin see: Shaolin Temple.

Shaolinquan Chinese martial art coming from the Shaolin Temple.

Shaolin Temple a Chan Buddhist monastery located in Henan Province, China. Dating back 1500 years, it is now well known for its martial arts training.

Shaoyang Lesser Yang. A term from Chinese acupuncture.

Shaoyin Lesser Yin. A term from Chinese acupuncture.

She Snake.

She Hu Shoot Tiger. A Taijiquan move.

Shen spiritual energy, spirit, psyche. SometimeS translated as "the soul", though many texts use the special terms Hun and Po. Shen refers to consciousness, the mental functions, the psychological processes and the immaterial aspects of the organism. In Qi Gong, it is said that the Shen resides at the Upper Dantian (third eye).

Shen Bu Shou She literally "the spirit is not kept at its residence", meaning abstracted, drifting off or restless.

Shen Fa body method, meaning strengthening and loosening exercises.

Sheng Tai see: Shen Tai.

Shenji Palace old term used for Upper Dantian.

Shen Ming deities, gods.

Shen Qi Xiang He literally "Shen and Qi are compatible". A term in Qi Gong practice.

Shenshu acupuncture point 23 on the Bladder meridian (Bl-23), translated as Kidney Shu.

Shen Tai immortal/spiritual/holy embryo. Also called Sheng Tai.

Shen Xi literally "spirit breathing".

Shen Xian Daoist immortal.

Shen Xian Yi Ba Zhua the Immortal One Seizes Once. A Taijiquan move.

Shen Xin Ping Heng balance of body and heart/mind.

Shen Xi Xiang Yi Shen and breathing are interdependent. A term in Qi Gong practice.

Shen Zhi literally "spirit will", meaning consciousness or state of mind.

Shen Zhi Bu Qing to be mentally confused.

Shen Zhu acupuncture point 12 on the Governing channel (Gv-12), translated as Body Pillar.

She Shen Xia Shi Snake Creeps Down or Downward Single Whip. A Taijiquan move.

Shi
1.   ten (10).
2.   to begin.
3.   form, style, type, pattern.

Shiatsu a Japanese massage method that involves pressing fingers on acupuncture points for therapeutic effect.

Shibashi Qi Gong a set of eighteen Tai Chi Qi Gong exercises, created by Lin Hou Sheng in 1979.

Shielding the Heart with the Sabre see: Hu Xin Dao.

Shi Er Duan Jin Twelve Pieces of Brocade. See: Ba Duan Jin Gong.

Shi Er Jing the Twelve Primary Qi Channels/Meridians in Traditional Chinese Medicine: Liver (Li), Gallbladder (Gb), Heart (Ht), Small Intestine (SI), Spleen (Sp), Stomach (St), Lung (Lu), Large Intestine (LI), Kidney (Ki), Bladder (Bl), Pericardium (Pc), and Triple Burner (San Jiao, SJ).

Shi Er Zhuang Twelve Postures. A style of Qi Gong training.

Shi Fu (Cantonese: Sifu). See: Qi Gong master.

Shi Ji Records of the Grand Historian. A historical book written around 94BC. It also covers the age of the legendary Yellow Emperor.

Shi Li literally "testing force". Moving exercises trained in Yiquan.

Shi San Shi thirteen postures or powers of Taijiquan consisting of Ba Men (8 doors or 8 basic moving patterns) and Wu Bu (5 steps). Shi San Shi is sometimes used as an old name for Taijiquan.

Shi San Shi Lao Jia Thirteen Posture Old Frame.

Shi Qi Food Qi, also called Grain Qi (Gu Qi). The Qi that comes from food and diet.

Shi Zhi Bai Lian Waving Lotus. A Taijiquan move.

Shi Zi Dao Pi Kan Xiong Huai Forming a Cross with the Halberd and Splitting the Heart or Crossed Glaive cuts Chest. A Taijiquan move.

Shi Zi Jiao crossed feet. A Taijiquan move.

Shi Zi Shou Cross Hands. A Taijiquan move.

Shi Zi Tui Cross Kick. A Taijiquan move.

Shi Zi Yi Dao Wang Ju Qi Forming a Cross with the Halberd then Raise or Pose with a Raised Blade. A Taijiquan move.

Silberstorff, Jan (born 1967) a German Taijiquan master, disciple of Chen Xiaowang.

Shoot Tiger see: She Hu.

Shoot Tiger With Bow see: Wan Gong She Hu.

Shou hand.

Shouhui Pipa Play the Pipa. A Taijiquan move.

Shoulder strike see: Kao.

Shou Shen means to keep oneself pure or to preserve one's integrity. A term in Qi Gong meditation.

Shoushi closing (stance). A Taijiquan move.

Shou Tou Shi With the head of a beast or Beast Head Pose or Animal Head Pose. A Taijiquan move.

Shu to count.

Shuai Jiao (Chinese) Wrestling.

Shuang Double.

Shuang Bai Lian Double White Lotus. A Taijiquan move.

Shuang Feng Guan Er Strike/Attack Ears with Both Fists or Twin Fists Strike Opponents Ears. A Taijiquan move.

Shuang Jin Jiao Double Pound Mortar. A Taijiquan move.

Shuang Tui Shou Push with Both Hands. A Taijiquan move.

Shuang Xiu Double Cultivation. See also: Xing Ming Shuang Xiu.

Shuang Zhong Double Weighting.

Shui Water. One of the Five Elements (Wu Xing). Associated with Kidneys and Bladder.

Shui Lu water way/path. A meditation method.

Shun to obey, to follow, to go along with.

Shun Bu Shuang Tui Shou Double Push Hands.

Shun Hu Xi natural breathing: the abdomen expands during inhalation and retracts during exhalation.

Shun Lan Zhou Hitting with Elbow. A Taijiquan move.

Shuowen Jiezi an ancient Chinese character dictionary.

Shu Xi to count the breath.

Si four (4).

Si Da Jie Kong literally "four large are empty". A Buddhist term, meaning the four elements are vanity. Also translated as "this world is an illusion".

Side bow stance see: Ce Gong Bu.

Side Lower Punch see: Wo Di Pao.

Sifu Cantonese spelling of Shifu. See: Qi Gong master.

Silk Reeling see: Chan Si Gong.

Single Leg Stance see: Du Li Bu.

Single Whip see: Dan Bian.

Sink Chest and Raise Back see: Han Xiong Ba Bei.

Si Qi Dead Qi, also called Gui Qi (Ghost Qi). The Qi remaining in a dead body. The opposite of Huo Qi (Fire Qi).

Sitting on crossed legs stance see: Zuo Pan Bu.

Sitting Stance see: Zuo Bu.

Six liu (6).

Six Desires see: Qi Qing Liu Yu.

Six Excesses (also Pathogenic Factors or Six Evils) a term used in Traditional Chinese Medicine for six climate forces that can cause disease: wind, summer heat, cold, dryness, dampness, and fire.

Six Healing Sounds see: Liu Zi Jue.

Si Xiang Four Phases or Four Manifestations, from which the Bagua (Eight Trigrams) evolved.

Six Sealing and Four Closing see: Liu Feng Si Bi.

Sixty-Four Hexagrams see: Yi Jing.

Skanda see: Wei Tuo.

Skin Breathing see: Fu Xi.

Small Catch and Push see: Xiao Qin Na.

Small Catching and Hitting see: Xiao Qin Da.

Small Circulation see: Xiao Zhou Tian.

Small Frame see: Xiao Jia.

Small Intestine Yang organ associated with the element Fire. Short form SI for Small Intestine meridian.

Small Nine Heaven see: Xiao Jiu Tian.

Snake Creeps Down see: She Shen Xia Shi.

Snake Spits out Tongue see: Bai She Tu Xin.

Sneak Step see: Dao Cha Bu.

Soaring Crane Qi Gong a Qi Gong form.

Song relaxation, loosening, letting go of unnecessary tension. See also: Fang Song.

Song Dynasty (960-1279) a dynasty in Chinese history.

Song of 13 postures a Taijiquan classic referring to the basic movements of Taijiquan (Shi San Shi).

Sound the heavenly drum see: Ming Tian Gu.

Sparrow Dashes Earth Dragon see: Que Di Long.

Spear see: Qiang.

Spirit see: Shen.

Spiritual Qi Gong see: Jing Shen Qi Gong.

Spleen Yin organ associated with the element Earth. Short form Sp for Spleen meridian.

Spread Arms Twice and Strike see: Dao Cha Dao Cha.

Spread Wings see: Zhan Chi.

Squeeze see: Ji.

Staff (weapon) Gun.

Stance see: Bu.

Standard Bow Stance see: Zheng Gong Bu.

Standing Meditation see: Zhan Zhuang.

Stationary Qi Gong see: Jing Gong.

Steel Finger see: Jin Gang Zhi.

Steel Wrapped in Cotton see: Gang Bao Mian Hua.

Step see: Bu.

Step Back and Repulse Monkey see: Dao Juan Gong.

Step Back and Ride the Tiger Tui Bu Kua Hu.

Step Back and Spread Arms see: Xia Bu Kua Gong.

Step Back and Strike with Elbow see: Tui Bu Ya Zhou.

Step Back and Whirl Arms like a Coiling Thread see: Dao Juan Hong.

Step Back to Wrap with Forearm see: Xia Bu Kua Gong.

Step Backward with the Back Foot see: Tui Bu.

Step Backward with the Front Foot see: Che Bu.

Step Forward with the Back Foot see: Shang Bu.

Step Forward with the Front Foot see: Jin Bu.

Stepping Backward into Riding Stance see: Xia Bu Kua Gong.

Stepping Backwards with Turning Arms see: Dao Juan Gong.

Stepping Forward Three Steps see: Shang San Bu.

Stomach Yang organ associated with the element Earth. Short form St for Stomach meridian.

Strange Organs the brain and uterus are referred to as "strange" as they are not linked to any organ or meridian.

Straight and Centered see: Zhong Zheng.

Straight Punch on the Head see: Dang Tou Pao.

Strike Down with the Fist see: Zai Chui.

Strike Ears with Both Fists see: Shuang Feng Guan Er.

Strike Tiger see: Da Hu Shi.

Strike with Full Arm see: Da Gong Quan Xiao Gong Quan.

Striking with Concealed Fist see: Yan Shou Gong Quan.

Strong Man Pounds the Mortar see: Jin Gung Dao Dui.

Suan Ming Chinese fortune-telling.

Subduing the Tiger see: Fu Hu.

Sui
1.   to follow.
2.   marrow.

Sui dynasty (581-618) a dynasty in Chinese history.

Sui Xi can mean "to follow the breath" (a meditation technique) or can mean "brain/marrow breath" (a Qi Gong breathing technique).

Sun braces three things see: Ri Tao San Huan.

Sun Cunzhou (1893-1963) a Sun style Taijiquan master, son of Sun Lutang.

Sun Jianyun (1914-2003) a Sun style Taijiquan master, daughter of Sun Lutang.

Sun Lutang (1860-1933) founder of Sun style Taijiquan. Also known for his skills in Xingyiquan and Baguazhang, he learned Taijiquan from Hao Weizhen.

Sun Shurong (1918-2005) a Sun style Taijiquan master.

Daughter of Sun Cunzhou and granddaughter of Sun Lutang.

Sun Simiao (died in 682) a Chinese doctor who wrote the books Beiji Qian Jin Yao Fang (consisting of 5300 recipes for medicine) and Qian Jin Yi Fang (consisting of recipes and health exercises).

Sun Style a Taijiquan family style created by Sun Lutang (1860-1933).

Sun Tzu (5th century BC) a Chinese general, military strategist, and philosopher. Credited as the author of the Art of War.

Sun Wanrong (born 1927) a Sun style Taijiquan master. Daughter of Sun Cunzhou and granddaughter of Sun Lutang.

Sunzi see: Sun Tzu.

Su Qin (380-284BC) an influential political strategist in ancient China. Mentioned in the move "Su Qin Bei Jian".

Su Qin Bei Jian Su Qin Bears Sword. A Taijiquan move.

Su Wen short name of the book Huang Di Nei Jing Su Wen.

Swallow pecks the soil see: Yan Zi Zhuo Ni.

Swallow separates its Golden Wings see: Yan Bie Jin Shi.

Sweeping Kick see: Ca Jiao.

Sweeping Legs see: Sao Tang Tui.

Sweep the Lotus see: Bai Lian.

Swing over Lotus see: Bai Lian.

Swing Step see: Bai Bu.

Swing the Foot and Drop Down see: Bai Jiao Die Cha.

Sword see: Jian.

T

Tai Chi see: Taiji.

Tai Chi Chuan see: Taijiquan.

T'ai Chi Ch'üan see: Taijiquan.

Tai Chi Qi Gong see: Shibashi Qi Gong.

Tai Chi Yang Sheng Zhang a Qi Gong form based on a Tai Chi stick form.

Tai Chong acupuncture point 3 on the Liver meridian (Li-3), translated as Great Surge.

Taiji literally "great pole". A philosophical concept meaning the oneness before duality, from which Yin and Yang originate. The Yin Yang symbol is called Taijitu.

Taiji Chu Shi opening movement.

Taiji Huan Yuan Return to Taiji. A Taijiquan movement.

Taiji Men Taiji familiy/school of thought. See also: Pai.

Taijiquan (Wade-Giles: T'ai Chi Ch'uan) literally "Taiji fist", meaning a Chinese internal martial art based on the theory of Taiji. It consists of complex choreographies of flowing, graceful movements and can be practiced for health, meditation, and self-defense. Major Taijiquan styles include, for example, Chen style and Yang style.

Taijitu the Yin Yang symbol.

Tailbone see: Weigu.

Tai Shang Lao Jun literally "Grand Supreme Elderly Lord". A name sometimes used for Laozi.

Tai Xi Embryonic/fetal Breathing, sometimes called Bi Qi (stopping the breath). The aim is to make the breath so relaxed, soft, effortless, quiet, and internal, that a feather held under the nose would not move (thus resembling the breath of a child in the womb).

Taiyang Greater Yang. A term used in acupuncture.

Taiyang martial stylists a school of Chinese martial arts credited with the creation of Huo Long Gong Qi Gong.

Taiyin Greater Yin. A term used in acupuncture.

Taizuquan a Chinese external martial art.

Taking up the stab-weapon, redirect it and dodge it see: Ying Feng Gun Bi.

Tang dynasty (618-907) a dynasty in Chinese history.

Tantien see: Dantian.

Tan Zhong (also Dan Zhong) acupuncture point 17 on the Conception vessel (Cv-17), translated as Middle of Chest. It is located in the center of the chest on the sternum.

Tao (also Dao) literally "path, road, method, way". According to Laozi's Tao Te Ching, the Tao is the underlying natural order and flowing course of the universe. It is also used for the spiritual path within oneself, with others, and with nature.

Tao Hong-Jin (456-536) a doctor and Qi Gong master who compiled the book Yang Shen Yan Ming Lu (Records of Nourishing the Body and Extending Life).

Taoism (also Daoism) a religious or philosophical tradition from China which advocates living in harmony with the Tao. As a religion it includes various sects, monasteries, and a complex ritual tradition. Daoism as a philosophy emphasizes simplicity, effortless action and naturalism to achieve peace, harmony, and longevity. Taoism was a big influence on the development of Chinese art, medicine, and Qi Gong.

Tao Jia literally "Tao family", meaning Taoism.

Taolu routine, pattern, form. A sequence of choreographed martial moves to simulate an attack or defense. Practicing forms is a key training method in traditional Chinese martial arts.

Tao Te Ching (also Dao De Jing) literally "Way Power/Virtue Classic". A Chinese philosophical text said to be created by Laozi. It is the basis of Taoism.

Tao Yin see: Dao Yin.

TCM see: Traditional Chinese Medicine.

Ten shi (10).

Test see: Yong Fa.

Testing force see: Shi Li.

Third Eye see: Yin Tang.

Thirteen Postures/Powers of Taijiquan see: Shi San Shi.

Three san (3).

Three Fierce Steps forward to frighten Xu Chu see: Shang San Dao Xia Sha Xu Chu.

Three Foundations see: San Ben.

Three Gates three core areas on the spine with significance for Taijiquan. The lower gate is at the lumbar vertebrae 3 (related to Ming Men), the middle gate is at the thoracic vertebrae 3 (related to Shen Zhu), and the upper gate is at the cervical vertebrae 1 (related to Feng Fu).

Three Kingdoms a historical novel set 169-280AD in China. It is acclaimed as one of the four great classical novels of Chinese literature.

Three Origins see: San Yuan.

Three Powers see: San Cai.

Three Steps back to frighten Cao Cao see: Xia San Dao Jing Tui Cao Cao.

Three Steps Forward see: Shang San Bu.

Three Treasures see: San Bao.

Three Upward Movements see: Shang San Dao Xia Sha Xu Chu.

Thrusting Vessel see: Chong Mai.

Thrust Kick see: Chong.

Thrust slantwise up and down see: Shang Xia Xie Ci.

Thunder style see: Hu Lei Jia.

Tian heaven or sky. Earth (Di), Heaven (Tian) and Man (Ren) are the "Three (Natural) Powers" (San Cai).

Tian Qi literally "Heaven Qi", meaning weather.

Tian Ren He Yi oneness of heaven and humanity. The theory that man is an integral part of nature.

Tian Shi the right time, destiny, heaven's natural order (e.g. seasons, months, days, hours).

Tian Zong acupuncture point 11 on the Small Intestine meridian (SI-11), translated as Celestial Gathering.

Tiao
1. to jump.
2. to harmonize, to regulate.

Tiao Jing to harmonize Jing.

Tiaokou acupuncture point 38 on the Stomach meridian (St-38), translated as Ribbon Opening.

Tiao Qi to regulate Qi.

Tiao Shen to regulate the spirit.

Tiao Xi to regulate the breath.

Tiao Xin to regulate the emotional mind.

Ti Er Qi Double Jump Kick. A Taijiquan move.

Tie Shan Iron Shirt. Martial art exercises to toughen externally and internally in order to protect the human body from impacts in a fight. Similar to Jin Zhong Zhao.

Tie Zhang Iron Palm. Hard style martial arts exercises for the palms.

Tiger Hu.

Tiger Leaps Suddenly see: Yi Peng Hu Jiu Di Fei Lai.

Tiger Pouncing on its Prey see: E Hu Pu Shi.

Tiger's Mouth see: He Gu.

Tiger Step Gong see: Hu Bu Gong.

Ti Jin raising/uprooting power.

Tile Hand see: Wa Shou.

Ting to listen, to hear.

Ting Jin the ability to accurately listen to/feel/interpret the energy and strength of another person.

Ting Xi to listen to the breath. A meditation technique.

Ti Shou Raise or Lift Hands. A Taijiquan move.

Ti Xi body breathing or skin breathing (Fu Xi), meaning using the entire body to breath Qi through the skin.

Ti Zhen Zhi literally "to understand truth and rest".

Toe-in-step see: Kou Bu.

Toe-out-step see: Bai Bu.

Tong Guan literally "to pass through frontiers/gates". Meaning the opening of gates or blockages and allowing Qi to flow freely through the channels.

Tong Jin literally "to interpret (the opponent's) strength". A term used in push hands practice.

Tong Ren Yu Xue Zhen Jiu Tu "Book of Needles and Moxa and the Points of the Bronze Man". A book written by Wang Wei-Yin around 1026.

Tong San Guan "to pass through the three gates". A term used in Qi Gong.

Tornado Kick see: Xuan Feng Jiao.

Tranquil Qi Gong see: Jing Gong.

Traditional Chinese Medicine a methodology of medicine developed in ancient China. Its therapeutic interventions focus on regulating the Qi. It includes acupuncture, moxibustion, herbalism, dietetics, massage, and Qi Gong.

Tree hugging stance see: Chang Bao.

Trembling Power see: Dou Jin.

Trinity Pole Standing see: Santi Shi.

Triple Burner see: San Jiao.

Triple Forward Move of the Halberd and Force Cao Cao Back see: Xia San Dao Jing Zu Cao Cao.

Tsai see: Cai.

Tsa Jiao see: Ca Jiao.

T-Step see: Ding Bu.

T.T. Liang (Tung Tsai Liang (1900-2001) a Taijiquan master, student of Cheng Manching.

Tu Earth. One of the Five Elements (Wu Xing). Associated with Stomach and Spleen. See also: Di.

Tu Di student, apprentice, disciple.

Tu Gu Na Xin to get rid of the old and bring in the new: to breathe out stale air and breathe in fresh. See also: Qi Gong.

Tui to push. See: Tui Shou.

Tui to retreat, to move back. See: Tui Bu.

Tui Bu Step Backward with the back foot. Also named Hou Tui. One of the five basic steps (Wu Bu).

Tui Bu Kua Hu Step Back and Ride the Tiger or Retreat to Ride Tiger. A Taijiquan move.

Tui Bu Ya Zhou Step Back and Strike with Elbow. A Taijiquan move.

Tui Na literally "to push and grasp". Chinese massages and therapeutic bodywork for healing and injury treatment. When combined with Qi Gong, it is called Qi Gong Tui Na.

Tui Shou push hands, also called listening hands or sensing hands. A two-person training routine in Taijiquan. It shows the connection between the Taijiquan form movements and the self-defense techniques. Different methods of Tui Shou are Dingbu, Shunbu, Hebu, and Houbu.

Tu Mai see: Du Mai.

Tu Na deep breathing.

Tuo Qian Jin Carrying a Thousand Pounds or Hand holds up a thousand kilograms or Hand supports one thousand pounds. A Taijiquan move.

Tuo Tian Supporting the Heavens. A term used in Qi Gong exercises.

Turn and Raise Glaive to Test the Water see: Fan Shen Zai Ju Long Tan Shui.

Turn around and double forward elbow see: Hui Tou Jing Lan Zhi Ru.

Turn around and Chop downward see: Fan Shen Xia Pi Jian.

Turn Back and Wave Double Lotus Kick see: Zhuan Shen Shuang Bai Lian.

Turn Back Quickly see: Shan Tong Bei.

Turn Body see: Zhuan Shen.

Turn Body and Hack to Bottom see: Wu Hua Sa Shou Wang Xia Kan.

Turn Body and Hack to Top see: Wu Hua Sa Shou Wang Shang Kan.

Turning Around Forearm Punches see: Hui Tou Dang Men Pao.

Turning body, boldly holding up someone with the feet see: Wu Hua Shang Jiao Shui Gan Zu.

Turning body, placing the halberd exactly to bottom right see: Wu Hua Wang You Ding Xia Shi.

Turning the body and performing a strike see: Fan Shen Kan.

Turn right to chop see: You Fan Shen Kan.

Twin Fists Strike Opponent's Ears see: Shuang Feng Guan Er.

Twisted Step see: Ao Bu.

Two er (2).

Types of Qi Gong names differ, but the most common types of Qi Gong are Health/Medical Qi Gong, Longevity/Vitality Qi Gong, Intellectual/Scholarly Qi Gong, Martial/Warrior Qi Gong, Spiritual Qi Gong.

U

Uncarved Block in Daoism it represents the original nature before conditioning, experience, and learning have happened. The aim is to return to that state of naturalness.

Universal Post see: Gong Shou.

Upper Burner see: Shang Jiao.

Upper Dantian see: Shang Dantian.

V

Varja a Sanskrit word meaning both thunderbolt and diamond. Also a weapon won in battle which is used as a ritual object.

Varja turns around and pestles see: Hui Tou Jin Gang Dao Dui.

Vessel see: meridian.

Vibration technique see: Dou Jin.

W

Wade Forward and Twist Step see: Qian Tang Ao Bu.

Wade-Giles a Romanization system for Mandarin Chinese. It was used in English books published until the 1970s. In mainland China it has been replaced by the Pinyin system (approved in 1958). In Wade-Giles it is Ch'i Kung and T'ai Chi Ch'üan, in Pinyin Qi Gong and Taijiquan.

Wai Dan External Alchemy, specifically the ingestion of plant- and/or mineral based pills or substances. See also: Lian Dan.

Wai Gong external work. Exercises that focus on physical body training.

Wai Jia literally "external family", meaning external martial arts (also Waiquan). In contrast to internal martial arts (Nei Jia), Wai Jia put greater emphasis on strength and conditioning exercises.

Wai Jin literally "External Power".

Wai Qi Zhi Liao Healing by external Qi projection or External Qi Healing. It refers to the projection of Wai Qi by a therapist for the purpose of leading a client's Qi back to a healthy, balanced state.

Waiquan see: Wai Jia.

Wai Shen External Kidneys, refers to the testicles. See also: Nei Shen.

Waist see: Yao.

Waist-level blade grinds around coiled roots see: Mo Yao Dao Hui Tou Pan Gen.

Wai Tai Mi Yao "Secret Essentials of an Outer Official". A Chinese medical book written by Wang Tao (702-772).

Wake the Qi see: Qi Shi.

Walking Obliquely see: Xie Xing.

Walking Qi Gong see: Guolin Qi Gong.

Wa Long Zhang tile palm. See also: Wa Shou.

Wang Fan-An a Chinese doctor who wrote the book Yi Fan Ji Jie.

Wang Mao Zhai (1862-1940) a Wu style Taijiquan master. One of Wu Quanyou's three primary disciples. One of his disciples was Yang Yuting.

Wan Gong She Hu Shoot Tiger with Bow or Bend Bow Shoot Tiger. A Taijiquan move.

Wang Maozhai (1862-1940) one of the primary disciples of Wu Quanyou.

Wang Tao (702-772) a Chinese doctor and Qi Gong master who wrote the book Wai Tai Mi Yao.

Wang Wei-Yi a Chinese doctor who published the book Tong Ren Yu Xue Zhen Ji Tu in 1026 AD.

Wang Xian (born 1944) a Chen style Taijiquan master.

Wang Xiang Zhai (1885-1963) a Chinese Xingyiquan master and founder of Yiquan. Also known as Nibao, Zhenghe or Yuseng.

Wang Zu-Yuan a Chinese doctor who edited the book Nei Gong Tu Shuo in 1881.

Wan Hua reeling flowers or rolling patterns in Tui Shou practice.

Ward off see: Peng.

Wa Shou Tile Hand. A hand form in Taijiquan, curved like a Chinese roof tile.

Water see: Shui.

Watts, Allan (1915-1973) a British philosopher, known as an interpreter of Eastern philosophy for the Western audience.

Wave Hands like Clouds see: Yunshou.

Waving Hands see: Da Gong Xiao Gong Quan.

Waving Lotus see: Shi Zhi Bai Lian.

Waving the curtain, stepping back, the enemy cannot find an opportunity see: Juan Lian Dao Tui Nan Zhe Bi.

Wearing the Frame see: Pi Jia Zi.

Wei Boyang (lived around 142AD). A Chinese author and alchemist who wrote the book Zhou Yi Can Tong Qi.

Weigu coccyx, tailbone. The corresponding acupuncture point is Chang Qiang (Gv-1).

Wei Mai see Yin Wei Mai or Yang Wei Mai.

Wei Qi Protective/Defensive/Guardian Qi. The Qi at the surface of the body that protects the body from negative influences, external pathogens, and disease: an energetic immune system.

Wei Tuo also known as Skanda. A warrior who protects Buddha relics, Buddhist teachings or a specific temple.

Wei Tuo presenting a pestle see: Wei Tuo Xian Chu.

Wei Tuo Xian Chu Wei Tuo presenting a pestle. A Taijiquan move.

Wei Zhong acupuncture point 40 on the Bladder meridian (Bl-40), translated as Bend Middle.

Whirlwind Kick see: Xuan Feng Jiao.

Whirlwind Withers the Flowers see: Feng Juan Can Hua.

White ape drags glaive and cuts upward see: Bai Yuan Bao Dao Wang Shang Kan.

White ape presents fruit see: Bai Yuan Xian Guo.

White clouds cover the head see: Bai Yun Gai Ding.

White crane spreads its wings see: Bai He Liang Chi.

White snake spits out tongue see: Bai She Tu Xin.

Whole Cannon Fist see: Quan Pao Chui.

Wide Bow Stance Yu Gong Bu.

Wild Goose Qi Gong see: Dayan Qi Gong.

Wild horse leaps the stream/over the brook see: Ye Ma Tiao Jian.

Wild horse parts mane see: Ye Ma Fen Zong.

William C.C. Chen (born 1935) A Taijiquan master and a disciple of Cheng Manching.

Wipe the Brow Palms see: Mo Mei Gong.

Wisdom Healing Qi Gong see: Zhineng Qi Gong.

With the head of a beast see: Shou Tou Shi.

Wo Di Da Zhuo Pao Punching from Bottom to Top. A Taijiquan move.

Wo Di Pao Punch Downward or Side Lower Punch. A Taijiquan move.

Wood (Mu) One of the Five Elements (Wu Xing). Associated with Liver and Gallbladder.

World Tai Chi Qi Gong Day celebrated every last Saturday in April (10am-12am) all over the world since 1999. Brought to life by Bill Douglas.

Wrapping Fire Crackers see: Guo Bian Pao.

Wu five (5).

Wu martial, military.

Wu shaman, witch, wizard. A practitioner of Shamanism.

Wu Bu five basic steps or directions of Taijiquan: Qianjing, Hou Tui, Zuo Gu, You Pan, and Zhongding. Can also be called Chin, Tui Bu, Ku, Pan, Ting. They are part of the thirteen powers of Taijiquan (Shi San Shi).

Wu Chi see: Wuji.

Wudang (Mountains) a small mountain range in the northwestern part of Hubei, China. Home to Taoist temples and monasteries, it is believed that a number of martial arts such as Taijiquan were created in this area. It is the Taoist counterpart to the Buddhist Shaolin Monastery.

Wude literally "martial morality/virtue/goodness", meaning Martial Code of Conduct.

Wugong see: Wushu.

Wu/Hao style a Taijiquan style created by Wu Yuxiang.

Wu Hua Martial Flower.

Wu Hua Fan Shen Wang Shang Kan Turn Body and Hack to Top. A Taijiquan move.

Wu Hua Sa Shou Wang Shang Kan Turn Body and Hack to Top. A Taijiquan move.

Wu Hua Sa Shou Wang Xia Kan Turn Body and Hack to Bottom. A Taijiquan move.

Wu Hua Shuang Jiao Shui Gan Zu Turning the body,

boldly holding up someone with the feet. A Taijiquan move.

Wu Hua Wang You Ding Xia Shi Turning body, placing the halberd exactly to bottom right. A Taijiquan move.

Wuji literally "no extreme". A concept in Chinese philosophy. Meaning the no extremity, undifferentiated emptiness before a beginning, preceding Taiji. Also used as a name for the beginning pose of a Taijiquan form.

Wu Jianquan (1870-1942) also Wu Chien-Chuan. Founder of Wu style Taijiquan. His father Wu Quanyou was a student of Yang Luchan and Yang Panhou. His daughter Wu Yinghua was married to Ma Yueliang.

Wuji Qi Gong Primordial Qi Gong. A Qi Gong form said to be developed by Zhang Sanfeng.

Wu Kuang-yu (born 1946) a Wu style Taijiquan master. Current head of the Wu family.

Wu Kung-i (1898-1970, also Wu Gongyi) a Wu style Taijiquan master. Grandson of Wu Quanyou.

Wu Kung-tsao (1902-1983, also Wu Gongzao) a Wu style Taijiquan master. Grandson of Wu Quanyou.

Wu Long Bai Wei Black Dragon sways/wags its Tail. A Taijiquan move.

Wu Nian Zhi Nian "the thought of no thought".

Wu Qi Chao Yuan literally "five Qis toward the origins". Meaning to keep the Qi of the five Yin organs at the original level. The idea is that being neither too Yang nor too Yin will slow down degeneration.

Wu Qin Xi Five Animal Sport. A set of medical Qi Gong exercises. Developed during the Han dynasty (202 BC-220 AD). It imitates the movements of animals. Depending on the specific set, the animals differ: tiger, deer, monkey, bear, bird/crane, tiger, dragon, leopard, snake.

Wu Quanyou (1834-1902) a Taijiquan master whose son Wu Jianquan is the founder of Wu style Taijiquan. Wu Quanyou was a military officer cadet in the Forbidden City in Beijing.

Wu Shou-Yang (1552-1640) a Chinese Qi Gong master.

Wushu literally "martial technique" or "military skill". A common name for the Chinese martial arts, mostly used for "modern martial arts". Other terms are: Zhongguo Wushu (Chinese martial techniques), Wu Yi (martial arts), Wugong (martial Gongfu), Guoshu (national techniques), and Gongfu (energy-time). Chinese Martial arts are divided into Internal Martial Arts (Neijia, e.g. Taijiquan, Baguazhang, Xingyiquan) and External Martial Arts (Waijia, e.g. Eagle Style, Praying Mantis).

Wushu Qi Gong Martial Arts Qi Gong. Qi Gong exercises practiced to improve skills in Chinese martial arts (e.g. power, flexibility, balance, coordination, speed).

Wu Style a Taijiquan family style created by Wu Quanyou.

Wuwei literally "non-doing" or "non-action", meaning doing without doing or behaving in a completely natural, uncontrived way. A fundamental concept of Taoism.

Wu Xin Five centers, meaning face, Laogong points on both palms and Yongquan points on both feet.

Wu Xing Five Elements. Also translated as Five Activities, Five Phases, Five Energetic Constellations, Five Networks. The Five elements consist of Wood (Mu), Fire (Huo), Earth (Tu), Metal (Jin), and Water (Shui). Phases, seasons, climates, colors, emotions etc. can be attributed to the Five Elements, e.g. the stages of transformation (birth, growth, maturity, decay, death). Within Traditional Chinese Medicine, these five elements must be balanced for health. See also: Creation Cycle and Destruction Cycle.

Wu Yi Martial Arts. See also: Wushu

Wu Yinghua (1907-1996) a Wu style Taijiquan master.

Granddaughter of Wu Quanyou. She was married to Ma Yueliang.

Wu Yuxiang (1812-1880) student of Yang Luchan. Founder of Wu/Hao style Taijiquan.

X

Xi
1. breath.
2. happiness, delight.

Xia down, downwards.

Xia Bu Kua Gong Stepping backward into riding stance or Step back to wrap with forearm or Step back and spread arms. A Taijiquan move.

Xia Bu Kua Hu Crouch step astride the tiger. A Taijiquan move.

Xia Dantian Lower Dantian, located in the lower abdomen below the navel. Associated with Qi. This point is known as Qi Hai (Sea of Qi) in acupuncture.

Xia Jiao lower burner, located in the lower abdomen. See also: San Jiao.

Xian immortal. Can mean a Daoist sage or a person who has attained enlightenment.

Xiang Gong Fragrance or Aromatic Qi Gong. A Qi Gong form.

Xian Ren Zhi Lu the Immortal Points the Way. A Taijiquan move.

Xian Tai Holy Embryo.

Xian Tian Qi Pre-Birth Qi, Pre-Heaven Qi, Prenatal Essence, Inherited Essence. The Qi that is acquired from the parents at conception and during gestation. It is stored in the Kidney and not replenishable.

Xiao filial piety, meaning the virtue of respect for one's parents, elders and ancestors.

Xiaohai acupuncture point 8 on the Small Intestine meridian (SI-8), translated as Small Sea.

Xiao Jia small frame. A style within Chen style Taijiquan.

Xiao Jiu Tian Small Nine Heaven. An old Taoist routine, credited as one of the predecessors of Taijiquan.

Xiao Lu Small Rollback. A Taijiquan move.

Xiao Qin Da Grasping and Hitting, also: small catching and hitting. A Taijiquan move.

Xiao Qin Na Small catch and push. A Taijiquan move.

Xiao Zhou Tian Small Circulation (literally "small heavenly circle"). An advanced Nei Dan Qi Gong technique in which Qi is circulated through the Conception and Governing Vessels.

Xia San Dao Jing Tui Cao Cao Triple Forward Move of the Halberd and Force Cao Cao Back or Three Steps Back to Frighten Cao Cao. A Taijiquan move.

Xia Shi see: She Shen Xia Shi.

Xie diagonal, slant, oblique.

Xie Bu Rest Stance.

Xie Gong Bu Diagonal Bow Stance.

Xie Fei Shi Diagonal Flying. A Taijiquan move.

Xie Xing Inclined/Diagonal/Oblique Posture or walking obliquely. A Taijiquan move.

Xie Xing Ao Bu Walking Obliquely Twist Step. A Taijiquan move.

Xin Heart, also meaning emotional mind or intention.

Xing (human) nature, character.

Xing Jin Shape Jin, meaning the power that can be seen physically.

Xing Ming Shuang Xiu "xing and ming practiced simultaneously". Daoist approach to cultivate/develop both the mind and the body.

Xing Qi moving Qi. See also: Qi Gong.

Xingyiquan literally "form intention fist". An internal martial art that is said to have been created by Yue Fei (1103-1142). It is based on five basic motions related to the Five Elements (Wu Xing), as well as motions corresponding to the twelve animals.

Xin Jia new frame. A style within Chen style Taijiquan. See also: Zhao Bao Jia.

Xinmen fontanelle (gap between the bones of an infant's skull).

Xin Nian literally "believe think", meaning faith, belief, conviction.

Xin Shen literally "heart spirit", meaning (state of) mind or psychic constitution.

Xin Shen Bu Ning literally "heart-spirit not peaceful", meaning being anxious and preoccupied, being distracted, wandering in thought.

Xin Xi Xiang Yi literally "heart and breathing are interdependent".

Xin Yi literally "heart mind", meaning the intention to do something that comes both from emotion and thought.

Xin Yuan Yi Ma literally "heart monkey mind horse" or "heart like a frisky monkey, mind like a cantering horse". Meaning to be hyperactive or to have ants in one's pants.

Xi Sui Jing literally "washing marrow/brain classic", usually translated Marrow/Brain Washing Classic or Bone Marrow

Cleansing. A Qi Gong form originated in the Shaolin monastery, with Da Mo often being credited as the creator.

Xiu Qi literally "cultivate Qi", meaning to protect, maintain, and refine Qi.

Xiu Shen Si Ming literally "cultivate body and await doom/death".

Xi Yuan Zhi literally "to tie the origin and stop". A meditation technique.

Xu empty, unoccupied, void.

Xuan Feng Jiao Tornado Kick or Whirlwind Kick. A Taijiquan move.

Xu Bu Empty Stance or Insubstantial Stance.

Xu Chu (died ca. 230) a bodyguard to Cao Cao, portrayed in the Three Kingdoms novel. He was described as big and strong. Mentioned in the move Shang San Dao Xia Sha Xu Chu.

Xue
1. blood.
2. cavity, hole, acupuncture point. Points along the skin where the Qi channels (meridians) come closest to the surface of the body. They are used in traditional Chinese medicine to encourage the circulation of Qi and blood, to affect particular organs and the organism as a whole.

Xuehai acupuncture point 10 on the Spleen meridian (Sp-10), translated as Sea of Blood.

Xu Kong void, hollow, empty.

Xun one of the Eight Trigrams. See: Bagua.

Xun Jin Kou Xue capturing nerves and pressure points.

Xu Wu nothingness.

Y

Yama King of Hell, also called Yan Luo. A wrathful god in East Asian and Buddhist mythology.

Yan Bie Jin Shi the Swallow separates its golden wings. A Taijiquan move.

Yang
1.　one half of the two symbolic polarities Yin and Yang (see also Taiji). The Chinese character means the sunny slope of a mountain. Yang is the active, warm, creative, solar, expansive, and masculine principle of Chinese philosophy.
2.　itching. See also: Ba Chu.

Yang Ban Hou see: Yang Pan Hou.

Yang Chiao Mai see: Yang Qiao Mai.

Yang Fu Kui see: Yang Luchan.

Yan Gao Shou Di literally "eyes high hands low", meaning to have high standards but little ability.

Yang Chengfu (1883-1936) a Yang style Taijiquan master. He was the grandson of Yang Luchan and son of Yang Jian Hou. His brother is Yang Shao-Hou. One of his students was Cheng Manching.

Yang Chien-Hou see: Yang Jian Hou.

Yang Heel Vessel see: Yang Qiao Mai.

Yang Jian Hou (1839-1917, also: Yang Chien-Hou). A Yang style Taijiquan master. Son of Yang Luchan and father of Yang Chengfu. His brother was Yang Pan Hou.

Yang Jun (born 1968) grandson of Yang Zhen Duo.

Yang Ling Quan acupuncture point 34 on the Gallbladder meridian (Gb-34), translated as Yang Mound Spring.

Yang Linking Vessel see: Yang Wei Mai.

Yang Luchan (also Yang Fu Kui; 1799-1872) founder of Yang Style Taijiquan. He learned his Taijiquan from Chen Changxing. His main disciples were Yang Pan Hou, Yang Jian Hou, and Wu Yuxiang.

Yang Pan Hou (1837-1890) a Yang style Taijiquan master. Son of Yang Luchan. One of his students was Wu Quanyou.

Yang Organs see: Fu.

Yang Qi can mean to raise/support/cultivate Qi or oxygen.

Yang Qiao Mai Yang Heel Vessel. One of the Eight Extraordinary Channels (Qi Jing Ba Mai).

Yang Quan Yang Fist, sometimes used for Yang style Taijiquan.

Yang Shao Hou (1862-1930) a Yang style Taijiquan master. Son of Yang Jian Hou, studied also with his uncle Yang Pan Hou.

Yang Shen to raise/support/cultivate the spirit.

Yang Shen Fu Yu Brief Introduction to Nourishing the Body. A book about the San Bao (Jing, Qi, Shen), written by Chen Ji Ru during the Qing dynasty.

Yang Sheng to maintain good health. See also: Qi Gong.

Yang Shen Jue Life Nourishing Secrets. A medical book written by Zhang An-Dao during the Song, Jin, and Yuan dynasties (960-1368).

Yang Shen Yan Ming Lu Records of Nourishing the Body and Extending Life, also translated as Records of Prolonging (One's) Destiny Through Nourishing Life. A Chinese medical book written by Dao Hong-Jin.

Yang Shou-Chung (1910-1985, also Yeung Sau Chung or Yang Zhen Ming). a Yang style Taijiquan master, son of Yang Chengfu. His three disciples are Ip Tai Tak, Chu Gin Soon, and Chu King Hung.

Yang style Taijiquan a Taijiquan family style founded by Yang Luchan.

Yang Wei Mai Yang Linking Vessel. One of the Eight Extraordinary Channels (Qi Jing Ba Mai).

Yang Yuting (1887-1982) a teacher of Wu style Taijiquan. He was Wang Mao Zhais primary disciple.

Yang Zhao Xiong see: Yang Shao Hou.

Yang Zhen Duo (born 1926) a Yang style Taijiquan master, son of Yang Chengfu. Current head of the Yang family.

Yang Zhen Guo (born 1928) a Yang style Taijiquan master, son of Yang Chengfu.

Yang Zhen Ji (born 1921) a Yang style Taijiquan master, son of Yang Chengfu.

Yang Zhen Ming see: Yang Shou Zhong.

Yan Luo see: Yama.

Yan Shou Chui Screen Hand and Punch. A Taijiquan move.

Yan Shou Gong Quan Hand Conceals Arm and Fist or Hidden Thrust Punch or Striking with Concealed Fist. A Taijiquan move.

Yan Zi Zhuo Ni Swallow pecks the Soil. A Taijiquan move.

Yao waist, lower back, loins. Used for the entire pelvis, abdomen and lumbar spine including its surrounding tissue.

Yao Lan Zhou Dragging the Waist and Hitting with the Elbow. A Taijiquan move.

Yao Zhan Bai She Cutting through the White Snake's Hip or Cut the White Snake at the Waist. A Taijiquan move.

Yecha Yaksha, a nature spirit.

Yecha explores the sea see: Ye Cha Tan Hai.

Yecha stretches towards the sea see: Ye Cha Tan Hai.

Ye Cha Tan Hai the flesh-eating demon explores the sea or Yecha explores the sea or Yecha stretches towards the sea. A Taijiquan move.

Yellow Dragon Stirs the Water Three Time see: Huang Long San Jiao Shui.

Yellow Emperor see: Huang Di.

Yellow Emperor's Classic of Internal Medicine see: Huang Di Nei Jing Su Wen.

Yellow Yard see: Huang Ting.

Ye Ma Fen Zong Part the Wild Horse's Mane or Wild Horse parts mane. A Taijiquan move.

Ye Ma Tiao Jian Wild horse leaps the stream/over the brook. A Taijiquan move.

Yeung Sau Chung see: Yang Shou-chung.

Yi
1. intention, thought, idea. The aim within Taijiquan is to set a mind intention (Yi) and let that direct the movement of Qi.
2. one (1).
3. justice, righteousness, friendship.
4. rippling. See also: Ba Chu.

Yi Chu Zuo Yi leads/moves Qi.

Yielding see: Rou.

Yi Fan Ji Jie "The Total Introduction to Medical Prescriptions". A Chinese medical book written by Wang Fan-An in the Qing dynasty.

Yi Jing (also I Ching or I Ging) Book/Classic of Changes. An ancient divination text and Chinese classic, more than 2500 years old. The Yi Jing consists of 64 hexagrams formed by combining the eight trigrams (Bagua) in different combinations.

Yi Jing Hua Qi to transform Jing into Qi.

Yi Jin Jing muscle/tendon change classic or muscle/tendon change transformation. A Qi Gong form originated from the Shaolin monastery, its creation credited to Da Mo around 500AD.

Yi Liao Qi Gong Medical Qi Gong. A type of Qi Gong to treat illness, often combined with other therapies such as acupuncture, massage and herbal tonics. See also: types of Qi Gong.

Yi Lu first form. A Chen style Taijiquan form within the old frame (Lao Jia).

Yin one half of the two symbolic polarities Yin and Yang (see also Taiji). The Chinese character means the shady slope of a mountain. Yin is the passive, cold, receptive, lunar, retracted, and feminine principle of Chinese philosophy.

Yin Chiao Mai see Yin Qiao Mai.

Ying hard, stiff, strong, firm.

Yingchuang acupuncture point 16 on the Stomach meridian (St-16), translated as Breast Window.

Ying Feng Gun Bi taking up the stab-weapon, re-direct it and dodge it or rolling away from the blade. A Taijiquan move.

Ying Gong Hard Gong, also called Hard Gongfu or Iron Palm.

Ying Jin Hard Jin. A type of Jin where the power comes mainly from the muscles. See also: Ruan Jin.

Ying Qi nutritive Qi, also called Nutritive Essence, Food Qi, Food Essence.

Ying Qi Gong Hard Qi Gong, also called hard Gongfu. Training that emphasizes physical strength and power. It uses dynamic or strenuous ways of conditioning the body, e.g. rib hitting, iron shirt (Tie Shan) or iron palm (Tie Zhang).

Ying Xiong Dou Zhi Eagle and Bear Vie with their Wits or eagle and bear fight. A Taijiquan move.

Yin Heel Vessel see: Yin Qiao Mai.

Yi Nian idea, thought.

Yin Linking Vessel see: Yin Wei Mai.

Yin Organs see: Zang.

Yin Qiao Mai Yin Heel Vessel. One of the Eight Extraordinary Channels (Qi Jing Ba Mai).

Yin Tang an acupuncture point located between the eyebrows, translated as Hall of Impression or Hall of Seal. Also known as the "third eye" area.

Yin Wei Mai Yin Linking Vessel. One of the Eight Extraordinary Channels (Qi Jing Ba Mai).

Yin Xu an archeological site of one of the ancient capitals of China. Source of the discovery of oracle bones and oracle bone script with Chinese writing.

Yin Yang see: Taiji.

Yin Yang meridians see: Shi Er Jing.

Yi Peng Hu Jiu Di Fei Lai Tiger Leaps Suddenly. A Taijiquan move.

Yip Tai Tak see: Ip Tai Tak.

Yi Qi Hua Shen literally "use Qi to change into Shen", meaning to nourish Shen with Qi.

Yiquan literally "mind-boxing", also called Da Cheng Quan (Great Achievement/Success Boxing). It was founded by Wang Xian Zhai and consists mainly of Zhan Zhuang and Shi Li.

Yi Shen Yu Qi literally "to use Shen to govern/manage Qi". A Qi Gong technique.

Yi Shi "Yi recognize", meaning to use Yi to sense and understand a situation. See also: Gan Jue.

Yi Shou Dan Tian literally "keep Yi in lower Dantian". Meaning, in Qi Gong training one should always lead the Qi back to the lower Dantian before ending the session.

Yi Tang She Crouch Step like a Snake creeping out from a House. A Taijiquan move.

Yi Yi Hui Shen to use Yi to meet the body.

Yi Yi Yin Qi to use Yi to lead Qi.

Yiyuanti literally "mind origin body", a term in Zhineng Qi Gong.

Yi Zhi will, willpower, determination.

Yi Zhi Chan One Finger Zen. A Qi Gong training technique. See also Jin Gang Zhi.

Yong Fa literally "use rule", meaning usage. The application of a Chinese martial art move to test its practical use.

Yong Quan acupuncture point 1 on the Kidney meridian (K-1), translated as Bubbling Well or Gushing Spring. It is located in the center of the foot and an essential point for self-massage and meditation.

You right (as opposite to left/zuo).

You Bo Cao Xun Shen ploughing the grass and searching for a snake (right) or parting the grass on the right side to search for the snake. A Taijiquan move.

You Ca Jiao rub with right foot. A Taijiquan move.

You Chong right thrust kick. A Taijiquan move.

You Deng Yi Gen Kick with right heel or Right stomp – one root. A Taijiquan move.

You Fan Shen Kan Turn right to Chop or turning the body and performing a strike (right). A Taijiquan move.

You Pan Look to the Right. One of the five basic steps (Wu Bu).

You Tuo Qian Jin Carrying a Thousand Pounds (right). See also Tuo Qian Jin.

Yu desire, appetite, passion.

Yuan dynasty (1271-1368) a dynasty in Chinese history.

Yuan source, origin.

Yuan Hou Tan Guo see: Bai Yuan Xian Guo.

Yuan Jing Original Essence. The essence inherited from the parents.

Yuan Qi Original Qi. The Qi inherited from one's ancestors and created from the Original Essence (Yuan Jing). It forms the basis of one's constitution.

Yuan Qiao literally "original hole", meaning important acupuncture points for Qi Gong.

Yuan Shen original Shen.

Yuan Shi Tian Zun the Primeval Lord of Heaven, a Taoist

deity.

Yu Bei (Shi) Preparation. A Taijiquan move.

Yue Fei (1103-1142) a Chinese military general who is associated with the creation of Xingyiquan and Ba Duan Jin Qi Gong.

Yu Gong Bu Wide Bow Stance.

Yu Huang Da Di Great Emperor of Jade, a mystical god in Chinese culture.

Yun even, well-distributed, uniform.

Yung Fa see: Yong Fa.

Yun Shou Cloud Hands or Wave Hands like Clouds. A Taijiquan move.

Yu Nü Chuan Suo Fair Lady works with Shuttles or Jade Maiden Shuttles back and forth. A Taijiquan move.

Yu Zhen acupuncture point 9 on the Bladder meridian (Bl-9), translated as Jade Pillow. It is located at the back of the head.

Z

Zai Chui Punch Down or Strike down with the Fist. A Taijiquan move.

Zai Ju Qing Long Kan Si Ren literally "next lift green dragon see dead people", meaning Raise glaive and survey the doomed. A Taijiquan move.

Zang Yin organs, also known as the "solid" organs" that store the Essences of the body (e.g. tears, sweat, saliva, mucus, and sexual secretions). The Yin Organs are the Liver, Heart, Spleen, Lung, and Kidney. Though not an organ, the Pericardium is also considered to be a Zang.

Zang Fu Organ Networks. In Traditional Chinese Medicine, an organ refers not only to an anatomical entity, but it is additionally related to tissues, activities, fluids, and meridians. See also: Zang or Fu.

Zen (Buddhism) The Japanese name for Chan (Buddhism).

Zero (0) ling.

Zhai Xing Huan Dao Pluck the stars and rotate the constellations. A Taijiquan move.

Zhan Chi Spread Wings. A Taijiquan move.

Zhang palm of the hand or sole of the foot.

Zhang An-Dao a Chinese doctor who wrote the book Yang Shen Jue.

Zhang Daoling (34-156) a Daoist who is credited with founding the Way of the Celestial Masters sect to Taoism.

Zhang Men acupuncture point 13 on the Liver meridian (Li-13), translated as Camphorwood Gate.

Zhang Sanfeng (ca. 12th century, also Chang San Feng) a legendary Chinese Taoist who is said to be the creator of Taijiquan.

Zhang Yu one of the creators of the 24 form.

Zhang Zhong-Jing (150-219) a Chinese doctor who wrote the book Jin Kui Yao Lue.

Zhang Zihe (1156-1228) a Chinese doctor who wrote the book Ru Men Shi Shi.

Zhan Shou Chopping Hand. A Taijiquan move.

Zhan Zhuang literally "standing like a post", also called Pole Standing or Standing Meditation. One of the most important Neijia training methods. Many variations exist, e.g. Hu Yuan, Cheng Bao, San Ti Shi.

Zhao Bao Jia / Zhaobao Taijiquan a Taijiquan style influenced by Jiang Fa and Chen Qingping.

Zhao Fa literally "make move – rule", meaning a movement in martial arts.

Zhen one of the Eight Trigrams. See: Bagua.

Zhen Chuan authentic tradition or handed-down teachings, meaning the true transmission from a master to a disciple.

Zheng Fu Hu Xi Normal Abdominal Breathing. Also called Buddhist Breathing.

Zheng Gong Bu Standard Bow Stance.

Zheng Qi literally "right Qi" or righteousness, meaning pure Qi or righteous Qi.

Zhen Ren literally "real/true/genuine person". A Daoist spiritual master.

Zhen Xi literally "real/genuine breathing".

Zhi to stop.

Zhi Dang (Chui) Punch to the Groin or Pointing to the Crotch. A Taijiquan move.

Zhi Guan Fa Stop and Look Method. A meditation method.

Zhineng Qi Gong Wisdom Healing Qi Gong. A Qi Gong form.

Zhi Nian Fa Method of Stopping Thought. A Qi Gong meditation method.

Zhi Xin Zhi Restrain the Xin and Stop Method. A meditation method.

Zhong
1.   middle/center; China.
2.   heavy, weighty. See also: Ba Chu.
3.   loyalty.

Zhong Dantian Middle Dantian, located in the solar plexus area. Associated with Jin. Also called Hunyuan Palace.

Zhong Ding Central Equilibrium. It means being centrally balanced and firmly rooted. One of the five basic steps (Wu Bu).

Zhong Du acupuncture point 6 on the Liver meridian (Li-6), translated as Central Metropolis.

Zhong Fu acupuncture point 1 on the Lung meridian (Lu-1), translated as Central Treasury.

Zhong Guan Centered Look. A meditation technique.

Zhongguo Wushu literally "Chinese Martial Techniques", see also Wushu.

Zhong Jiao Middle Burner. One of the Triple Burners (San Jiao) in Chinese medicine.

Zhong Kui a figure in Chinese mythology, regarded as a guardian spirit who can tame ghosts and evil beings. His image, a fierce sword-wielding warrior, is often painted on household gates.

Zhong Kui holding/wields the sword see: Zhong Kui Zhang Jian.

Zhong Kui Zhang Jian Zhong Kui wields/holding the sword. A Taijiquan move.

Zhong Mai (also Chung Mai or Jung Mai) Central Channel. It is one of the Eight Extraordinary Channels (Qi Jing Ba Mai).

Zhong Pan Middle Tray. A Taijiquan move.

Zhong Qi central/middle Qi.

Zhongwan acupuncture point 12 on the Conception channel (Cv-12), translated as Central Venter.

Zhong Yang Guo Shu Guan Central Guoshu Institute. A Chinese martial arts institute, founded by the Chinese government in 1928 to promote Chinese martial arts.

Zhong Zheng literally "central/middle correct/proper", meaning fair & honest.

Zhou (also Chou) literally "elbow", usually used for elbow stroke. One of the eight basic methods of Taijiquan (Ba Men).

Zhou Di Chui Fist under Elbow. A Taijiquan move.

Zhou Di Kan Quan Fist showing under the elbow or Elbow Meets Fist. A Taijiquan move. Also Zhou Xia Kan Quan.

Zhou dynasty (1046BC-256BC) a dynasty in Chinese history.

Zhou Xia Kan Quan fist under elbow. A Taijiquan move. Also Zhou Di Kan Quan.

Zhou Yi Can Tong Qi (short: Cantong Qi) a book thought to be the earliest on alchemy in China, written by Wei Boyang.

Zhuang Zhou see: Zhuang Zi.

Zhuangzi (369BC-286BC) a Chinese philosopher credited

with writing the book Zhuangzi.

Zhuan Qi Zhi Rou literally "concentrate Qi, deliver soft", meaning to concentrate on Qi and achieve softness. A famous sentence from Laozi's Tao Te Jing.

Zhuan Shen Turn Body. A Taijiquan move.

Zhuan Shen Shuang Bai Lian Turn Back and Wave Double Lotus Kick. A Taijiquan move.

Zhuan Xin literally "to monopolize heart/mind", meaning to concentrate or concentration.

Zhu Bing Yuan Hou Lun "Thesis on the Origins and Symptoms of Various Diseases". An encyclopedia written by Chao Yuan-Fang. It comprises 50 volumes and 1739 entries of symptoms, including 260 different ways of increasing the Qi flow.

Zhu Dan Xi (1281-1358) a Chinese doctor who wrote several books, e.g. Ge Zhi Yu Lun.

Zhuo Li crude strength, brute force; also meaning to try really hard.

Zhu Tiancai (born 1944) a Chen style Taijiquan master.

Zi Wu Liu Zhu literally: "Zhi" (midnight), "Wu" (midday), "Liu Zhu" ("the flowing tendency"). Also called the midnight-moon ebb-flow or chronoacupuncture. A concept in TCM that the flowing and ebbing of Qi and Xue along different meridians is related to designated times during the day. Times are usually displayed in meridian clocks or meridian flow wheels.

Zou Huo Ru Mo literally "catch fire – enter the devil". A Chinese term traditionally applied to describe physiological or psychological disorders, which are believed to result from excessive or long-term incorrect (Qi Gong) practice.

Zuan to drill.

Zuo left (opposite to right/you)

Zuo Bo Cao Xun She ploughing the grass and searching for a snake (left) or parting the grass on the left side to search for the snake. A Taijiquan move.

Zuo Bu Sitting Stance.

Zuo Ca Jiao rub with left foot. A Taijiquan move.

Zuo Chong left thrust kick. A Taijiquan move.

Zuo Gu Beware of the Left. One of the five basic steps (Wu Bu).

Zuo Pan Bu sitting on crossed legs stance.

Zuo Wan Settle down the Wrist or seating the Wrist. A Taijiquan hand posture.

Zuo Wang see: Ru Jing.

Numbers

0 ling.

1 yi.

2 er.

3 san.

3 steps Forward see: Shang San Bu.

4 si.

4 phase/manifestations see: Si Xiang.

5 wu.

5 animals Qi Gong see: Wu Qin Xi.

5 centers see: Wu Xin.

5 elements or phases see: Wu Xing.

5 steps see: Wu Bu.

6 liu.

6 Healing Sounds see: Liu Zi Jue.

6 Sealing and 4 Closing see: Liu Feng Si Bi.

7 qi.

8 ba.

8 Basic Methods see: Ba Men.

8 Extraordinary Channels see: Qi Jing Ba Mai.

8 Pieces of Brocade see: Ba Duan Jin Qi Gong.

8 stances see: Ji Ben Ba Shi.

9 jiu.

10 shi.

12 Pieces of Brocade see: Shi Er Duan Jin Qi Gong.

12 primary channels see: Shi Er Jing.

12 routines from Daoyin tradition see: Daoyin Yang Sheng Gong Shi Er Fa.

13 postures/powers of Taijiquan see: Shi San Shi.

18 movements see: Shibashi Qi Gong.

24 form a Taijiquan form based on Yang style Taijiquan created in 1956 by Chu Guiting, Cai Longyun, Fu Zhongwen, and Zhang Yu.

37 form a Taijiquan form developed by Cheng Marching based on Yang style Taijiquan.

100 bai.

103 form a Yang style Taijiquan form.

108 form a Yang style Taijiquan form.

1000 qian.

CPSIA information can be obtained
at www.ICGtesting.com
Printed in the USA
LVOW10s1304060418
572569LV00022B/400/P